SpringerBriefs in Criminology

M000220370

Translational Criminology

More information about this series at http://www.springer.com/series/11178

Lorie A. Fridell

Producing Bias-Free Policing

A Science-Based Approach

 Springer

Lorie A. Fridell
Department of Criminology
University of South Florida
Tampa, FL
USA

ISSN 2192-8533   ISSN 2192-8541 (electronic)
SpringerBriefs in Criminology
ISSN 2194-6442   ISSN 2194-6450 (electronic)
SpringerBriefs in Translational Criminology
ISBN 978-3-319-33173-7   ISBN 978-3-319-33175-1 (eBook)
DOI 10.1007/978-3-319-33175-1

Library of Congress Control Number: 2016940801

Printed on acid-free paper

This Springer imprint is published by Springer Nature
The registered company is Springer International Publishing AG Switzerland

Acknowledgements

I am grateful to Jennifer Eberhardt of Stanford University who first introduced me to the science of implicit bias; that exposure changed the trajectory of my work. I also want to thank the many law enforcement professionals who, over the past 15 years, have shared their wisdom, ideas and stories that helped to produce the content of Chap. 3 of this book. I thank the following individuals who reviewed the book draft and provided helpful input: Chief Scott Cunningham of the Kernersville (NC) PD, retired LAPD Captain John Mutz, Lt. Scott Prell of the Cheektowaga (NY) PD, Captain Tony Raimondo of the Sanford (FL) PD, and Cheryl Staats of the Kirwan Institute for the Study of Race and Ethnicity. I am grateful to Cynthia Lum of George Mason University who provided me with the opportunity to write this book and then exercised great patience as I (slowly) produced it. And, finally, I thank my partner-in-life, Martin, who made sure I stepped away from my computer now and again to smell the roses.

This book is for all the "Nikki's" in the world. Nikki emailed me after she saw on the news that I had just completed a 2-day, science-based Fair and Impartial Policing training session in her jurisdiction. With a writing style reflective of the poor education she had received in her low income area, she shared her most recent experience with police, which was ugly. She ended her note with: "So thanks for trying to help them with their biased ways." I can't know whether she was on the receiving end of biased policing, but I have posted her email in my office nonetheless so I don't forget who has the greatest stake in fair and impartial policing.

This book is also for all the cops out there, the overwhelming majority of which are decent hard-working human beings who want to serve their communities to the best of their abilities. I hope this book about human biases will help them do just that.

Contents

About the Author

Dr. Lorie A. Fridell is a faculty member in the Department of Criminology at the University of South Florida (USF) in Tampa. Prior to joining USF in August of 2005, she served for six years as the Director of Research at the Police Executive Research Forum (PERF) in Washington, DC. Dr. Fridell has over 30 years of experience conducting research on law enforcement. Her primary research areas are police use of force and violence against police; she has also conducted recent research on police deviance and the effectiveness of body-worn cameras. Dr. Fridell is a national expert on biased policing. She speaks nationally on this topic and provides consultation and training to law enforcement agencies. Previous publications on this topic include two books: *Racially Biased Policing: A Principled Response* and *By the Numbers: A Guide for Analyzing Race Data from Vehicle Stops* (and the companion guide, *Understanding Race Data from Vehicle Stops: A Stakeholder's Guide*). With her partner Anna Laszlo, law enforcement practitioners, national experts on the psychology of bias, and funding from the US Department of Justice, she has developed five Fair and Impartial Policing training programs for local, state and federal law enforcement personnel (see www. fairandimpartialpolicing.com). She and her fellow trainers administer this training in the United States and Canada.

Chapter 1
Introduction

> *The profound implication of the discovery of implicit prejudice is that anybody is capable of prejudice, whether they know it or not, and of stereotyping, whether they want to or not.*
>
> (Hardin and Banaji, 2013, p. 23).

It is well documented that police intervene disproportionately with certain groups. Much of the research, for instance, has focused on the disproportionate intervention by police with racial and ethnic minorities (see e.g., Walker et al. 2000). Research has shown that this disproportionality is in evidence for various police activities such as arrests or tickets (e.g., Kochel et al. 2011; Langton and Durose 2013), use of force (e.g., Eith and Durose 2011; Engel and Calnon 2004; Smith 1986; Terrill and Mastrofski 2002), searches (e.g., Eith and Durose 2011; Gelman et al. 2007; Higgins et al. 2008, 2011; Langton and Durose 2013), pedestrian or vehicle stops (e.g., Engel et al. 2002; Gelman et al. 2007; Langton and Durose 2013; Lundman and Kaufman 2003), or Mobile Data Terminal (MDT) warrant inquiries (Meehan and Ponder 2002). There is also evidence of disproportionate intervention with, or otherwise differential treatment of, other groups by police based on age (e.g., Liederbach 2007; Rosenfeld et al. 2011), gender (e.g., Farrell 2015; Smith et al. 2006), socioeconomic status (e.g., Birkbeck and Gabaldon 1998), religion (Ammar et al. 2014), homelessness (e.g., Douglas 2011), residency status (Ammar et al. 2005; Davies and Fagan 2012), sexual orientation or gender identity (e.g., Amnesty International 2005; Bellafone 2013; Center for Constitutional Rights 2012; Demby 2012), disabilities (Bartley 2006; Chown 2010; Kewley 2001), and language abilities (e.g., Pisarski 1994), to name a few.

Two general explanations have been put forth to explain the overrepresentation of various groups, such as racial/ethnic minorities, among people with whom police intervene. Some have argued that the overrepresentation of racial and ethnic minorities in police interventions reflects the greater involvement of these groups in criminal behavior and police resistance (see e.g., Black and Reiss 1967; Bratton and Knobler 1998; Brown and Langan 2001; MacDonald 2001, 2003; Smith et al. 1984; White 2002). Another explanation is that this greater intervention is due to police bias and prejudice (Brown 1981; Chambliss 1994; Fyfe 1982; Jacobs and O'Brien

© The Author(s) 2017
L.A. Fridell, *Producing Bias-Free Policing*,
SpringerBriefs in Translational Criminology, DOI 10.1007/978-3-319-33175-1_1

1998; Sorenson et al. 1993).[1, 2] Regarding the latter, various theories have been put forth in the academic literature to characterize how bias might manifest in policing —and society more generally—to produce differential treatment (for reviews, see e.g., Engel et al. 2002; Leiber 2008; Tomaskovic-Devey et al. 2004; Warren et al. 2006). These include, for instance, racial threat, symbolic threat, attribution, liberation, focal concerns, and cognitive bias theories. Among the bias-explanations, the most widely cited by researchers and writers posits that officers act on the basis of their prejudicial attitudes (Engel et al. 2002).

Social scientists have been studying "prejudicial attitudes" since the 1950s and report that these attitudes come in different forms; they also report that the way bias and prejudice manifests in our society has changed over time (Schuman et al. 1997). These scientists distinguish between "explicit bias" and "implicit bias" and report that "our grandparents' prejudice" (Fiske 2008, p. 14) was more likely to be in the form of *explicit* bias and modern day bias is more likely to be *implicit.*

Explicit bias is generally what one envisions when thinking about prejudice and bias. With explicit biases, a person associates various groups with characteristics— mostly negative characteristics. These attitudes are based on animus or hostility toward the groups (Amodio and Mendoza 2010). As an example, a racist has explicit biases. A racist recognizes in himself animus or hostility towards a particular racial group, such as Blacks. This person could and would describe and justify this bias. The bias that this person has can impact behavior, producing discriminatory actions and the person is unconcerned about this impact (Devine 1989; Dovidio et al. 1996; Plant and Devine 1998).

As above, modern day bias is most likely to be in the form of *implicit* biases. Implicit biases are similar to explicit biases in that we link individuals to stereotypes or generalizations associated with their group or groups (e.g., groups based on gender, race, LGBT status). These biases can impact perceptions and behavior producing discriminatory behavior (Dasgupta 2004; Dovidio et al. 2002; Kang et al., 2012; McConnell and Liebold 2001). But, unlike explicit biases, implicit biases are not based on animus or hostility and these "implicit associations" can impact perceptions and behavior *outside* of conscious awareness (Devine 1989; Petty et al. 2009). Even individuals who, at the conscious level, reject prejudice and stereotyping, can and do manifest implicit biases (Graham and Lowery 2004; Kang et al. 2012).

Hardin and Banaji (2013) point out that our discussions about, and interventions to address, bias in society have to catch up with what we know from the science. They report, "…personal and public policy discussions regarding prejudice and discrimination are too often based on an outdated notion of the nature of prejudice" (p. 13). This has certainly been true as pertains to the discussion of bias in policing

---

[1]A third explanation, that gets less attention, is that racial groups differ in the *nature* of their offending, rather than the *extent* of it. See e.g., Mitchell and Caudy (2015).

[2]The words "bias" and "prejudice" are used interchangeable in this book to denote the human tendency to "prejudge" individuals based on the characteristics or stereotypes associated with their group membership.

and this deficiency has been detrimental both to the national discussion and efforts to produce bias-free policing. Many police and community stakeholders have formed their views about biased policing based on their (outdated) understanding of how prejudice manifests in individuals. Knowing only about what we now label "explicit" biases, they have assumed that, to the extent there is bias in policing, it is produced by individuals with animus toward groups; the prejudice of these police professionals, they believe, is conscious and deliberate. That is, many in our society who are concerned about this issue, have assumed that officers with explicit biases, *and only officers with explicit biases,* produce bias in policing. This "old paradigm" (focusing only on explicit biases) needs to be replaced with the "new paradigm"—one in which we recognize that bias in policing, as in all of society, can be produced by either explicit *or* implicit bias.

Widespread acceptance of the old paradigm has been detrimental for three reasons. First of all, this characterization of bias in policing has produced distortions that have harmed the relationship between law enforcement and some of the diverse communities that they serve. There are subgroups of community members that believe that bias in policing is widespread—racial and ethnic minorities being a prime example (Carlson 2004; Drake 2014). If the individuals in these groups think that biased policing is widespread *and* if they believe, too, that it is produced only by individuals with explicit biases, they may well conclude that there are *a lot of* individuals in policing who have animus toward their groups and are consciously and deliberately acting upon that animus when they police. This produces a very negative picture of police personnel and has the potential to negatively impact community perceptions of agency legitimacy. Agencies need to be perceived as legitimate to effectively serve their communities (Tyler 1990, 2004; Tyler et al. 2015).

A second way the "old paradigm" has been detrimental is that it has produced distortions that lead police professionals to minimize the issue of biased policing and be very defensive about it. If police believe that biased policing is produced only by individuals with explicit biases, such as racists, and if they reject that they are themselves racist and see few or none around them, they may well decide that their agency and profession are being unfairly criticized about this problem, the occurrence of which, they believe, must be rare.

The third negative result of the belief that bias in policing is produced by individuals with explicit biases—and only by individuals with explicit biases—is the adoption of misguided interventions. Interventions that are based on outdated notions of how prejudice manifests in modern society would target only overt, intentional discrimination and ignore the well-meaning individuals in policing who have implicit biases. The traditional, "old paradigm" efforts might take the form of trying to change the hearts and minds of individuals thought to have animus toward groups and/or trying to identify individuals with overt, deliberate biased actions and holding them to account through discipline or even termination. Per Hardin and Banaji (2013, p. 14): "...an overemphasis on the bad apples may well be detrimental to considerations of policy because it assumes the problem of prejudice to be that of the few rather than that of the many."

The purpose of this book is to bring the modern science of bias to the profession of policing. This effort parallels similar ones occurring in other professions like medicine (see e.g., Gonzalez et al. 2014), the legal profession (e.g., National Center for State Courts, n.d.), and business (Lublin 2014) that have also historically dealt with bias based on outdated notions of how it manifests. In Chap. 2 of this book, I summarize the key research on implicit bias and discuss how implicit bias might manifest in the policing profession. Additionally, I examine the research on how individuals can reduce and manage their biases.[3] Chapter 3 of the book provides practical information for police leaders on how to facilitate bias-free policing within an agency—in light of our broader "new paradigm" perspective about how biased policing is produced.[4]

The importance of bias-free policing cannot be overstated. Biased policing is unjust. By definition, biased policing means that groups are being treated differently by police without justification. This is a violation of individual rights; specifically, it reflects a violation of the Equal Protection Clause of the U.S. Constitution. Biased policing can produce ineffective policing, such as when it leads police astray in their investigations and crime control interventions. Police may, for instance, focus on one particular group and miss the criminal behavior of another. Biased policing can have other serious consequences for both community members and police professionals. It can produce over-vigilance with certain groups that could have dire consequences for individuals. For instance, members of a group that is more likely than another to be arrested (despite similar behavior) face consequences such as incarceration, fines, and obstacles to employment and housing. Over-vigilance in the use of force, based on stereotypes about groups, can lead to unnecessary and/or unjustified deaths. Under-vigilance on the part of police may allow criminal wrongdoers to go free. Under-vigilance can also be unsafe; it can lead to officer injury or even death.

Perceptions of biased policing also have powerful consequences. When individuals or communities perceive the police to be biased in their application of the law, the police lose the legitimacy they need to do their work. Without it, individuals do not call the police to report crime; they do not provide police with the information they need to solve crimes. Without legitimacy, police professionals may not be believed by jurors evaluating their testimony in court. At the agency level, concerns of biased policing can lead to reduced budgets, calls for increased oversight, and demands for changes in leadership.

The consequences of both biased policing and the perceptions of it have played out quite visibly and powerfully since the events in Ferguson (MO) in August 2014,

---

[3]Comprehensive reviews of research on implicit bias are contained in three publications of the Kirwan Institute for the Study of Race and Ethnicity: *State of the Science: Implicit Bias Review 2013* and *State of the Science: Implicit Bias 2014*, both written by Cheryl Staats; and Staats et al. (2015) *State of the Science: Implicit Bias Review 2015*. These can be found at the Kirwan Institute web site at www.kirwaninstitute.osu.edu.

[4]An important additional audience consists of community stakeholders who, with this knowledge, can hold their law enforcement leaders to account.

which reignited the discussion of biased policing in the United States. It has been a painful period for police and community, with each new incident fanning the flames of community concern and exacerbating the feelings on the part of police of being besieged. But this "reignited discussion," however painful, offers an opportunity for greater understanding and significant change. It is my hope that this book will enhance both.

This is not a book for "agencies with issues." Consistent with the science of bias, this is a book for *any agency* that hires humans to do the work of law enforcement. Because police are human, they have biases; because they have biases, every agency needs to be proactive in producing bias-free policing. And, of course, it is better to start now, rather than to wait for problems to flare up. As Chief Cunningham, currently with Kernersville (NC) reports, starting now to implement these science-based efforts to promote bias-free policing "makes good business sense."

Chapter 2
The Science of Implicit Bias and Implications for Policing

The Science of Bias

As previewed above, modern bias is most likely to manifest as "implicit bias." Through our implicit biases, we link individuals to the stereotypes associated with their group(s). This can impact our perceptions and behavior and can occur even in individuals who, at the conscious level, reject bias, prejudice, and stereotyping.

The Characteristics of Implicit Bias

The key characteristics of implicit bias are as follows:

- We categorize individuals and link them to the stereotypes associated with their groups
- This can occur outside of conscious awareness
- Implicit biases can impact actions producing discriminatory behavior
- This can occur even in individuals who, at the conscious level, reject prejudice and stereotyping.

Bias starts with our automatic tendency to categorize individuals. We categorize individuals and objects to make sense of the world, which includes categorizing people according to group membership (based on e.g., gender, weight, race). We then attribute to these individuals the stereotypes associated with their group. The researchers have determined that these processes do not occur for all situations and people, but instead are most likely when we are facing "ambiguous stimuli." With regard to people, this means that categorizing individuals and linking them to stereotypes is most likely when we encounter people we do not know. These people come into our sphere as "blank slates" and we try to "fill in" that blank slate with information. To do this, we link them to groups to which they belong and then to

© The Author(s) 2017
L.A. Fridell, *Producing Bias-Free Policing*,
SpringerBriefs in Translational Criminology, DOI 10.1007/978-3-319-33175-1_2

the stereotypes associated with those groups. We are much less likely to "fill in" with stereotypes a person we already know; this person is already "filled in" with information.

One line of research has examined what categories, linked to personal characteristics, prompt implicit biases. These categories include ethnicity/race (e.g., Bertrand and Mullainathan 2004), gender (e.g., Axelson et al. 2010; Banaji and Greenwald 1995; Levinson and Young 2010), social class (e.g., Haider et al. 2011), sexual orientation (e.g., Hebl et al. 2013; Oberle et al. 2011), religion (e.g., Ahmed 2010; French et al. 2013; Park et al. 2009), body shape (e.g., Bessenoff and Sherman 2000; Schwartz et al. 2006; Teachman et al. 2003), and age (e.g., Gross and Hardin 2007; Levy 1996), to name a few. Another, broader categorization reflects our tendency to favor our own "in group" (see e.g., Brown and Zagefka 2005; Reskin 2005). According to Staats (2013, pp. 11–12): "As soon as we see someone, we automatically categorize him or her as either 'one of us', that is, a member of our ingroup, or different from ourselves, meaning a member of our outgroup…. By favoring ingroup members, we tend to grant them a measure of our trust and regard them in a positive light." What we perceive as an "in group" may vary by context; it may be based on race, profession, income, or other factors, depending on the situation (Allport 1954/1979).

Another line of research examines the types of stereotypes to which various groups (e.g., Asians, women, young people) are linked, such as insecurity (e.g., Bessenoff and Sherman 2000), kindness/compassion (Axelson et al. 2013; Bessenoff and Sherman 2000), selfishness (Bessenoff and Sherman 2000), musicality (Bessenoff and Sherman 2000), strength of memory (e.g., Levy 1996), enthusiasm (e.g., Axelson et al. 2013), speed of learning (Axelson et al. 2013), rebelliousness (e.g., Gross and Hardin 2007), moodiness (e.g., Gross and Hardin 2007), and danger or threat (e.g., Correll et al. 2007a; Correll et al. 2011).

As above, linking a group to a stereotype associated with that group does not require animus or hostility toward that group. In fact, scientists have determined that *mere knowledge* of the stereotype produces an implicit bias (Correll et al. 2002).

Our tendency to link individuals to the stereotypes associated with their group(s) is automatic and occurs outside of conscious awareness (see e.g., Devine 1989; Blair 2002; Dovidio et al. 2009; Rudman 2004). According to Devine's (1989) seminal article on the discovery of implicit bias,

> Automatic processes involve the unintentional or spontaneous activation of some well-learned set of associations or response that have been developed through repeated activation in memory. They do not require conscious effort and appear to be initiated by the presence of stimulus cues in the environment … A critical component of automatic processes is their inescapability; they occur despite deliberate attempts to bypass or ignore them (p. 6).

To adopt the language of author Malcolm Gladwell (2005), these are "blink responses"; they reflect our "thinking without thinking." Social scientist David R. Williams (as quoted in Wilkerson 2013, p. 134) refers to the automatic and outside-awareness character of implicit bias as "frightening," because implicit bias is "an automatic and unconscious process, (and) people who engage in this unthinking discrimination are not aware of the fact that they do it." The automatic nature of implicit biases is highlighted by research that has documented *physiological* man-ifestations of bias. Susan Fiske at Princeton documented differential brain activity using magnetic resonance imaging (MRI) when she showed subjects pictures of people who do not look homeless and pictures of people who do. There is a certain part of the brain that is "activated" when people think about themselves or other people and indeed, it lit up in Fiske's subjects when they were shown pictures of individuals who did not look homeless. But when the subjects were shown pictures of individuals who appeared to be homeless, this area of the brain was not activated; instead "within a moment of seeing the photograph of an apparently homeless man... people's brains set off a sequence of reactions characteristic of disgust and avoidance" (Fiske 2008: p. 15).

Implicit biases can impact actions—producing discriminatory behavior (Dasgupta 2004; Kang et al. 2012; Rooth 2007). In laboratory studies, the behavior that has been impacted by implicit biases ranges from "non-verbal friendliness" (e.g., Dovidio et al. 2002) to shooting (Correll et al. 2002, 2007a, b). Biases have been shown to impact employment decisions (for an overview, see e.g., Fiske and Krieger 2013), jury verdicts and sentencing (see Mitchell et al. 2005 for a meta-analysis), and medical treatment (e.g., Schulman et al. 1999; Weisse et al. 2001).

Implicit biases can manifest even in people who, at the conscious level, reject prejudice and stereotyping. As reported above, categorizing someone and linking him/her to the stereotypes associated with his/her group does not require animus; it only requires knowledge of the stereotype. This fact is consistent with the finding that our implicit associations do not necessarily line up with our conscious beliefs (see e.g., Banaji and Greenwald 1995; Beattie et al. 2013; Devine 1989; Gilbert and Hixon 1991; Kang et al. 2012; Macrae et al. 1994). In her seminal 1989 article, Devine wrote, "It would appear that the automatically activated stereotype-congruent or prejudice-like responses have become independent of one's current attitudes or beliefs" (p. 15). Describing one of the three studies presented in that article, she explains that, even for subjects who have no conscious prejudices towards a particular group, "activation of stereotypes can have automatic effects that if not consciously monitored produce effects that resemble prejudiced responses" (Devine 1989, p. 12).

This means that implicit biases occur even in individuals who, at the conscious level, reject prejudices, bias and stereotyping and explains the findings that even individuals in groups *subject* to stereotypes can have those same implicit biases (Greenwald and Krieger 2006; Reskin 2005). As Staats (2014, p. 17) explains, "(Although) we generally tend to hold implicit biases that favor our own ingroup... research has shown that we *can still hold implicit biases against our ingroup*" (italics added). One example is the finding that a pro-White bias is found even among non-Whites (see e.g., Dovidio et al. 2002) and, conversely, anti-Black biases are found among Blacks (see e.g., Correll et al. 2002; Nosek et al. 2002).[1] This latter finding is consistent with Jesse Jackson's statement, "There is nothing more painful to me … than to walk down the street and hear footsteps and start thinking about robbery, then look around and see somebody White and feel relieved."

This fact—that women can have biases against women, Blacks can have biases against Blacks, poor individuals can have biases against poor individuals, and so forth—is frequently lost in the conversation about bias in policing. For instance, in the wake of Ferguson—with an intensive focus on police use of force against Blacks—we seem to see increased emphasis placed on the race of the officer involved in such incidents. "The White officer and Black subject" is highlighted, seemingly to imply that the incident is linked to White biases against Blacks.[2] (Since the vast majority of police personnel in the country are White, we should not be surprised that any use-of-force incident involves a White officer.) Also, in the discussion of police bias, sometimes the call for agency diversity is seemingly touted as a way to hire people without biases. Again, this is misguided. There are, as discussed below, good reasons to have diversity within agencies, but the suggestion that "diverse individuals" are bias-free is contrary to the science.

Research on Implicit Biases Related to Crime and Aggressiveness

There are various methods that have been used to measure the activation of implicit biases in subjects (for a review, see Staats 2013). I will review these methodologies by providing examples from studies on the implicit biases that link demographic groups to crime and violence. Most of these studies have focused on the "Black-crime implicit bias" (or "Black-crime association") (see e.g., Fridell 2008); that is, these studies have examined the extent to which people associate Black people with street crime and violence.

One method that has been used to measure the Black-crime implicit bias— involves "priming." In such studies, the subject is exposed to an initial stimulus (the "prime") that is hypothesized to influence a subsequent response and thereby

---

[1]For instance, Correll et al. (2002) found that in a "shoot, don't shoot" task (see coverage of this methodology below) both White and African American samples shot Black targets more quickly than White targets and were more likely to erroneously shoot unarmed Blacks (versus unarmed Whites).

[2]That the race of the subject as Black is also emphasized by the press, is indicated in the 2015 document entitled "Unarmed Civilians and the Police." Street Cred reviewed 125 incidents in the first 8 months of 2015 in which police killed an unarmed civilian. In examining the press coverage of these incidents, they report that their analyses of 420 examples of press coverage, "the media mentioned the race of the decedent and the officer four times more when the decedent was Black" p. 7.

confirm (or disconfirm) an implicit bias. Eberhardt et al. (2004), for instance, assessed whether "priming" the subjects subliminally with Black male faces or White male faces impacted on the subjects' subsequent ability to identify degraded images of crime-related objects. The researchers argued that, if the Black-crime association exists, exposure to Black male faces during the priming phase of the study would make crime images more accessible. During the first ("priming") phase, subjects sat at computer screens; one-third was exposed subliminally to Black male faces, one-third was exposed to White male faces, and the control group was exposed to lines (i.e., no faces). In the second phase of the study, subjects saw a series of degraded objects on the computer screen that would quickly become clearer in small increments (41 frames). The subjects were instructed to push a certain computer key when they could identify the object and then report what the object was. The objects were either crime-related objects (e.g., gun, knife) or crime-neutral objects (e.g., camera, book). The speed of identification was recorded.

The results supported a strong Black-crime association. The subjects who had been subliminally primed with Black male faces were quicker than the subjects in the other two conditions to identify the crime-related objects. Interestingly, the subjects who had been subliminally primed with White male faces were *slower* than even the control group (no face prime) to detect crime-related objects. In sum, the study showed that *Blacks* and *crime* are concepts that are closely linked in our heads and that the concepts of *Whites* and *crime* are not.

Another methodology involves response latency measures (see e.g., Dovidio et al. 2009; Greenwald et al. 1998; Kang and Lane 2010; Rudman 2004). Staats explains (2013, p. 24): "These measures rely on reaction times to specific tasks in order to uncover individual's biases .... The underlying premise of these reaction-time studies is that individuals are able to complete cognitively simple tasks relatively more quickly than those that are mentally challenging." An example of a latency measure is the popular Implicit Association Test (IAT) that is available on line.[3] In taking the IAT, respondents are timed as they sort concepts. Since we are faster at completing simple tasks than challenging ones, we will be faster "sorting" concepts that are *linked* in our heads than sorting concepts that are *not linked*. As such, if a person is faster at linking "women" and "childcare" than "men" and "childcare," the implication is that the person has an "association" in his/her head between women and childcare (but not men and childcare). One example is the Black/White IAT, in which the respondents are directed to categorize White and Black faces with positive and negative words. As Staats explains (2013: p. 27), "Faster reaction times when pairing White faces with positive words and Black faces with negative terms suggests the presence of implicit pro-White/anti-Black bias."

Correll et al. (2002) used response time as one of their measures in exploring the Black-crime implicit bias. In their study, college student subjects were required to

---

[3]Go to https://implicit.harvard.edu/implicit/. An article evaluating the validity of the IAT is Jost et al. (2009).

determine very quickly (measured in milliseconds) whether the man pictured on the computer screen was a threat or not a threat. Some of the males were White and others were Black; they held either a gun or a "neutral" (i.e., nonthreatening) object. The subjects were instructed to push the "shoot" button if the person held a gun and the "don't shoot" button if he held a neutral object. Correll measured both time-to-decision (in milliseconds) and errors (shooting an unarmed person or failing to shoot an armed person) to see if the race of the target impacted perceptions of threat. Correll et al. (2002, p. 1325) hypothesized a Black-crime implicit bias; they expected participants to "respond with greater speed and accuracy to stereotype-consistent targets (armed African Americans and unarmed Whites) than to stereotype-inconsistent targets (armed Whites and unarmed African Americans)." The results supported a Black-crime implicit bias. The subjects shot an armed male more quickly if he was Black than if he was White. Conversely, they more quickly decided *not* to shoot an unarmed White than an unarmed Black. The most common *errors* were shooting an unarmed Black man and not shooting an armed White man (see also Plant and Peruche 2005).

Another line of studies takes advantage of the fact that our implicit biases are likely to manifest when a situation is ambiguous. In the classic "shove" study, subjects observed a video of two people interacting and then were asked questions about that interaction (Duncan 1976). In the video, subjects saw either a White or a Black person shove the other person; importantly, the shove was ambiguous—not clearly aggressive, but not clearly in jest. Indicating an implicit association between Blacks and aggression, the subjects labeled the ambiguous shove as more violent "when it was performed by a black than when the same act was perpetrated by a white" (Duncan 1976, p. 590). Other studies, too, have documented a widespread Black-crime implicit bias (Amodio et al. 2003; Amodio et al. 2004; Correll et al. 2006; Greenwald et al. 2003; Payne 2001; Payne et al. 2002).

It is important to acknowledge here (just as it is important to acknowledge this in the context of training police on this science) that stereotypes are based in part on fact. As an example, the Black-crime implicit bias or "blink response" is based in part on fact. As much as we shy away from saying it (at least in police-community circles), the truth is that people of color *are* overrepresented among the people who commit "street crimes" relative to their representation in the population.[4] Criminologists have conducted extensive studies regarding who commits crime and determined that socio-economic status is a key to the link between people of color and crime. They characterize the relationship as follows:

- Individuals of low socio-economic status are disproportionately represented among people who commit street crime (see e.g., Cullen and Gilbert 1982; Pratt and Cullen 2005; Sherman et al. 1989; Western 2002; Western et al. 2001).

---

[4]The phrase "street crime" is used here to encompass the behaviors with which municipal police usually deal–such as, robberies, prostitution, trespassing, and burglary, and to distinguish those from "crimes of the powerful" (e.g., tax fraud, insider trading, mortgage fraud).

- People of color are disproportionately represented among low-income individuals (see e.g., DeNavas-Walt and Proctor 2014; Lin and Harris 2009; Macartney et al. 2013).

Because of the above, it is not surprising, that researchers find that people of color are disproportionately represented among individuals who commit street crime (see e.g., Ellis 1988; Hipp 2011; Krivo and Peterson 1996; Kubrin and Weitzer 2003; McNulty and Bellair 2003; Ousey 1999; Sampson and Lauritsen 1997; Sampson et al. 2005; Vieraitis 2000).[5] But it is equally important to acknowledge that the actuality that stereotypes are based in part on fact does not justify the use of stereotypes in making policing decisions. Police err when they treat individuals as if they fit the group stereotype. Policing based on stereotypes can be ineffective, unsafe, as well as unjust.

The section above summarized research on the Black-crime implicit bias. And, indeed, in terms of stereotypes about *who commits crime*, it is the *Black-crime* implicit bias that has been the most studied. Some researchers, however, have started to extend the research to look at what *other* groups are stereotyped as criminal and thus reflected in implicit biases. Unkelbach et al. (2008) used the "shoot, don't shoot" methods described above to assess whether study subjects linked Muslims to threat. Subjects participated in a computer exercise wherein they were exposed to individuals who were either armed or unarmed and wearing Islamic headgear or not. The subjects were instructed to shoot at armed individuals, but not to shoot unarmed ones. The subjects had to respond very quickly, so that the experimenters were measuring their "blink" responses. As hypothesized, the subjects were more likely to shoot Muslim targets, even when the Muslim-looking targets were carrying nonthreatening objects—indicating a Muslim-threat implicit bias. These same researchers varied the targets by gender, too, and confirmed an implicit bias linking men to threat.[6]

Sadler et al. (2012) used the "shoot, don't shoot" methodology to see whether subjects responded differentially to Blacks, Latinos, Asians, and Caucasians. Their nonpolice subjects (their findings for the *police* subjects are provided below) evidenced a Black-crime implicit bias in their response times. The authors report (p. 295) that the "participants were especially likely to favor the 'shoot' response over the 'don't shoot' response when the target was Black rather than any other race."[7] These nonpolice subjects did not, however, react differently to Caucasians, Asians, or Latino targets.

---

[5]For an exception, see American Civil Liberties Union (2013).

[6]Highlighting the predominance of "in-group" versus "out-group" biases (that are linked to cultural differences), Schofield et al. (2015) found that Saudi Arabian subjects were more likely to shoot the White target than the Middle Eastern target.

[7]James et al. (2013) also tested a Hispanic-crime implicit bias using a variation of the shooting paradigm methodology. This research is covered under the discussion of "controlled responses".

Does Neighborhood Context Matter?

Are the findings that individuals are over-vigilant with Blacks (as seen in the "shoot, don't shoot" studies) moderated by the level of dangerousness of the neighborhood? Correll et al. (2011) have tested the impact of neighborhood context on the activation of implicit biases using laboratory, shoot-don't-shoot methods. According to their hypotheses, based on the theory of implicit bias, the bias towards shooting Blacks should be reduced or even *disappear* in dangerous contexts. Citing the model produced by Cacioppo and Berntson (1994), Correll et al. (2011) conjecture that "initial negative information has a powerful impact on behavior .... The incremental effect of each additional piece of negative information becomes less potent" (p. 185). The first component of this model—that negative information is weighted more heavily than positive information—reflects the well documented "negativity bias" (for an overview, see Baumeister et al. 2001). Applied to shoot-don't-shoot situations, the dangerous environment—the "initial negative information"—will have the powerful impact that will increase the likelihood that research subjects will shoot opponents; the fact that a subject is Black, however— the "additional piece of negative information"—will be less potent. The result would be a greater tendency to shoot in dangerous neighborhoods, but an elimination of the tendency to shoot Blacks *more than* non-Blacks. Correll et al's research results supported their hypothesis; in their laboratory study, the bias against Blacks (reflected in the subjects' errors and speed of decision-making) disappeared in dangerous contexts. One study using actual police use-of-force data produced results that were at least "consistent" with the hypothesis and laboratory results of Correll et al.[8] Using data from 1846 use-of-force incidents from a single jurisdiction, Fridell and Lim (2016) found that the finding of higher levels of force used against Blacks (even when controlling for key variables including level of resistance) disappeared in high crime areas. Additional research—both in the lab and in the field—is needed to further explore the potential impact of context on biases pertaining to threat.

Evidence of Implicit Biases in Police Subjects

Some of the recent research on implicit bias has examined how bias might manifest in various professions. As examples, research has been conducted examining how biases might manifest in medical professionals (see e.g., Stone and Moskowitz 2011; Van Ryn and Saha 2011), legal professionals (e.g., Levinson and Young 2010;

---

[8]This was not a "critical test" of the hypothesis.

Richardson and Goff 2013; Smith and Levinson 2012), and educators (e.g., Tenenbaum and Ruck 2007; Van den Bergh et al. 2010).[9]

Several teams of researchers have examined implicit biases in police subjects (e.g., Correll and Keesee 2009; Correll et al. 2007a, b; James et al. 2014; James et al. 2013, 2016; Sadler et al. 2012; for a review, see Correll et al. 2014). One line of research indicates that officers—like other people—have implicit biases that link racial/ethnic minorities to aggression, threat and violence. When the "shoot, don't shoot" methodology was implemented using police as subjects, Correll and colleagues found that police subjects (similar to non-police subjects) were quicker to shoot at armed Black targets than armed White targets, indicating "robust racial bias."

The findings of Sadler et al. (2012) for their *nonpolice* subjects were described above. Recall, they used the "shoot, don't shoot" methodology and included targets that were Black, Latino, Asian and Caucasian to determine which groups were and were not associated with threat. These researchers also included a subject pool comprised of *sworn law enforcement* personnel and, in their response times, the police manifested a Black-crime implicit bias when the response times to Black targets were compared to Latinos, Asians, and Whites. The police response times also indicated a Latino-crime implicit bias—when response times for Latinos were compared to those of Asians and Whites (not Blacks).[10] The results, in sum, indicated that Blacks were perceived as the most threatening of the four groups; Latinos were perceived as more threatening than both Caucasians and Asians, and Caucasians were perceived as more threatening than Asians. Regarding the police subjects, the researchers state, "our results suggest that Blacks and Latinos may be more stereotypically associated with violence than Whites and Asians" (p. 307). A Black-crime implicit bias in police subjects has also been documented by Eberhardt et al. (2004) and Plant and Peruche (2005).

The line of research presented in this section documents that police, like other humans, have implicit biases—such as the Black-crime and Latino-crime implicit bias. Further below, however, I will explore two other lines of research that add some important nuances to this set of findings. In the section on bias-reduction techniques, we will explore the "good news" research supporting state-of-the-art use-of-force training and the "bad news" research indicating that police may sometimes put themselves in danger out of fear of the consequences of using force against a racial/ethnic minority.

---

[9]Overview chapters on "Implicit Bias in Education," "Implicit Bias in Criminal Justice," and "Implicit Bias in Health/Health Care" are contained in Staats (2013), and updates are provided in Staats (2014) and Staats et al. (2015).

[10]With regard to *errors*, "the police officers were better able to distinguish weapons from non-threatening objects, when held by Black and Latino targets than by Asian and White targets" (pp. 306–307).

Implicit Bias and the Police Profession

So what are the potential costs of implicit biases that manifest in police professionals? Policing based on implicit biases and stereotypes can be, not just unjust, but ineffective and unsafe. It can lead officers to be over-vigilant with certain groups and under-vigilant with others. It can lead them to focus on one demographic group and therefore miss the individuals of other demographics who are committing crime. It can lead to poor tactics and investigations.

Several of the researchers have commented on how, for instance, the *Black-crime* association might manifest in the work of police. Peruche and Plant (2005) suggest that officers' implicit biases might increase the scrutiny of Blacks compared to others; it might lead to more searches of Blacks than others. According to Plant et al. (2005, p. 142):

> If a police officer possesses an expectation (i.e., stereotype) that Black people are more likely to be violent criminals than are White people, then split-second decisions about whether or not a suspect is an imminent threat could be biased and lead to more aggressive responses to Black compared to White suspects. For example, when deciding whether or not to fire on a suspect, if police officers expect that Black people are more likely to be an imminent threat than White people, then this may influence how they interpret and respond to situations involving Black suspects with tragic consequences.

Payne (2001), too, commented on the implications of the findings of his "shoot, don't shoot" study for the real world of policing:

> If the officer is like the average participant in our experiments, he or she will experience some degree of automatic bias when interacting with a Black suspect. That is, the officer will be more prone to respond as if a Black suspect is armed, compared to a White suspect (pp. 190–191).

This comment by Payne is consistent with analyses of officer-involved shootings by the Philadelphia Police Department (PPD). Fachner and Carter (2015) found that the shooting of unarmed Black individuals was more likely to be due to Threat Perception Failure (TPF) than was the case for shooting unarmed individuals of other races.[11] They defined TPF as "mistake of fact" shootings. In these situations, the officer perceives (reasonably or not) that the subject is armed when, in fact, s/he is not. This perception might be due to a misperception of an object (e.g., cell phone vs. gun) or actions (e.g., furtive movements). This finding is consistent with a Black-crime implicit bias. Also consistent with the science is their finding that the manifestation of TPF in incidents with Black subjects is unrelated to race of the officer.[12]

---

[11]To be precise, the researchers actually found the highest TPF with Asian subjects, but noted that the percentage was likely unreliable because of the small number of Asians that were subject to officer-involved shootings.

[12]The researchers found some differences across officer races (more Black and Hispanic officers experienced TPF), but these differences were not statistically significant.

All of the above examples point to the consequence of over-vigilance with Blacks compared to Whites, but the "shoot, don't shoot" studies (e.g., Correll et al. 2002, 2007b) also point to another potential consequence, under-vigilance. For instance, Correll et al., in both of the studies, found that police and nonpolice subjects alike were slower to identify a gun in the White man's hand. Groups that might be linked to "non-dangerous" stereotypes include Asians, well-dressed individuals, and the elderly. That those "non-dangerous" stereotypes might lead to under-vigilance is highlighted in a story shared by an officer with the Las Vegas Metropolitan Police Department (LVMPD).[13] The officer telling the story had responded to the scene near where two fellow officers, in 2014, had just been ambushed while eating lunch. The responding officers knew very little about who had killed their colleagues and where the killer(s) had gone, but civilians directed them to a nearby Walmart store. The officer telling the story was moving down an aisle toward a White male that he had identified as the active shooter when he saw a White female. He reports, "I thought that this woman wasn't going to be a threat and so I let her remain as she was a little bit longer than I should have." Once he realized that she "wants to be exactly where she is right now," he exchanged gunfire with the woman who, along with her male partner, had killed his colleagues. (She was injured, he was not hit.) This officer implies that his (very understandable, very human) stereotypes about who is dangerous slowed down his response—almost adding to the already tragic loss of the LVMPD.

Two back-to-back role plays that are part of the science-based Fair and Impartial Policing (FIP) Training Program highlight the potential danger to officers when they police based on stereotypes about groups.[14] In the first role play, "Woman with a Gun," two of the recruits get a dispatch telling them that a credible witness reports that there is a woman at a bus stop on the corner of Maple and 1st Street brandishing a firearm.[15] When the recruits enter the scene, there is a woman on the bus bench at the corner of Maple and 1st who matches the description (although no gun is apparent). As they start to interact with this woman, another female role player enters. She is talking in a very animated/agitated fashion, telling the first woman that a car that looks similar to the one belonging to the first woman's husband has been involved in a serious accident. She is insistent that they must go to the scene of the accident immediately. This woman is not threatening, but she is a significant distractor. The trainers let the recruits respond as they see fit and then they stop the role play.

---

[13]The story was shared during a segment entitled "Cops see it differently, Part 2" on "This American Life" broadcast February 13, 2015. Found on 9/15/2015 at http://www.thisamericanlife.org/radio-archives/episode/548/cops-see-it-differently-part-two?act=2#play. Relevant segment starts at 37:40; the officer's story starts at 54:00.

[14]The Fair and Impartial Policing Training Program will be covered in more depth in Chap. 3.

[15]This dispatch, by necessity, varies from location to location, depending on state gun laws. Whatever the wording, the dispatch will give the officers reasonable suspicion to detain and to frisk.

With no debrief, the second role play, "Man with a Gun," is implemented, which is identical to the first, except that it is a *man* with a gun and a man who serves as the distractor. In the overwhelming majority of the implementations, the recruits handle the woman with the gun differently from the man with a gun. The team dealing with the woman does not find the gun. (To reduce the concerns of a male police officer frisking a female suspect, the first team is mixed gender.) The second team of recruits is aggressive with the man and finds the gun through detention and frisk. It appears that the recruits handle this scene based on stereotypes/ generalizations about women; specifically, that women are not dangerous. As suggested above, we can recognize that stereotypes are based in part on fact; we can recognize that, generally, fewer women have guns than men. But, by treating this woman as if she matched the stereotype, the recruits show that *policing based on stereotypes/biases is unsafe.*[16]

Another role play as part of the FIP training makes the point that policing based on stereotypes can be ineffective. A pair of recruits in the class respond to a domestic violence call and are told the perpetrator is still on the scene. The dispatched trainees find the sobbing victim with a man on one side and a woman on the other; they are both patting the back of the victim saying, "I'm so sorry this happened. It will never happen again." Consistently, the recruits approach the man and ask to speak with him off to the side, and leave the lesbian partner—the abuser—with the victim.

The stereotypes that might impact police do not all have to do with perceived criminality or danger. Stereotypes might impact whether an officer, for instance, thinks a person is smart or not, or truthful or not, based on that person's visible characteristics. An officer might assume a Hispanic is undocumented or that a person with poor English speaking abilities is unintelligent. An officer might, at a two car crash where each driver has a different story, believe the man in the tie and BMW over the low income, young kid in a beat-up truck. Indeed, there are a vast array of police operational decisions at the line level[17] that might be impacted by biases—ranging from the relatively low level, low impact decisions such as with whom to engage in a consensual encounter to high-level, high-impact decisions, such as the decision to use deadly force. Some believe (and some department policies are written as if to imply) that we are only to be concerned about bias as pertains to decisions/actions that implicate the Fourth Amendment. As with the examples above, this is not the case. Biases could impact any of the infinite number of decisions (even "micro-decisions") that line-level officers make—some that implicate the Fourth Amendment and some that do not. Examples include

- Whom to watch, investigate as a "suspicious person" (whom to ignore)
- Of whom to determine immigration status prior to custodial arrest

---

[16]Police report that male gang members often give the guns to the females when they are together on the streets, presumably because they believe the police will be less vigilant with the females.

[17]In a subsequent section, I discuss how bias might manifest in the decisions of individuals at the higher levels of an agency. These include both operational and managerial decisions.

- What questions to ask ("Do you own this car?" "Are you on probation or parole?" "Where are you coming from?")
- Whether to search or from whom to request consent to search
- Against whom to use force or higher levels of force
- Whom to treat with dignity and respect.

As we learned above, the influence of bias on actions/decisions might be automatic and wholly outside conscious awareness. This is a critically important point, because some law enforcement personnel have assumed that they would *know* if bias was impacting them; and, based on this assumption, they have determined that they do not engage in biased policing.[18] How bias might be covert, rather than overt, was conveyed well in the California Commission on Police Officer Standards and Training (POST) training video on "Racial Profiling." The spokesperson (Anthony West of the Office of the California Attorney General) said:

> You'll never hear someone say 'I'm going to stop that person because they are Black or I'm going to stop that person because they've got an accent.' No one is going to say that. We don't think of ourselves in those terms. But you will find people who will say 'I'm going to stop those people because they seem like they're up to no good or they are up to something.' Or 'I'm going to stop that person because I know this part of town and I know how these people think.' 'These people' and 'up to no good' – these are all proxies for why we might act in a certain way around a particular group of people. (CA Commission on POST).

Biases might impact what officers refer to as their "gut reactions." It is true that officers see things that others do not and draw conclusions that others would not, based on their experience and training, but officers should consider that those "gut reactions" could *also* reflect, at least in part, their implicit biases. Why does that person seem suspicious to the officer? Is the officer picking up on behavioral cues and contextual elements that nonpolice would miss, or is she being impacted by the biases that we all have? Howard Ross, the author of *Everyday Bias: Identifying and Navigating Unconscious Judgments in our Daily Lives* cautions (2014, p. 147): "It is fine to listen to your 'gut,' but don't trust it without question!"

Several factors can facilitate the manifestation of bias. Increasing the likelihood of bias are situations that (1) involve discretionary activities, (2) are ambiguous, and/or (3) are fast moving. It is the discretionary activities on the part of police that are susceptible to bias; or, in other words, decisions for which officers have no discretion will not be impacted by their biases. An example of a non-discretionary activity is a search incident to a lawful arrest. While it is possible that the selection of the person for arrest was based on biases, once the arrest is made, the person *will be searched*. This search is non-discretionary and thus cannot be impacted by officer biases. In the same vein, if an agency has a 0 % or 100 % enforcement policy for certain situations, the implementation of the police activity at the line level (assuming adherence to the policy) will not be biased. If the agency has decided never to enforce possession laws for small amounts of marijuana or has

---

[18]In fact, research indicates that individuals who perceive themselves to be objective make more biased decisions than those who do not (Kang et al. 2012).

decided that every student on a campus with a knife (regardless of the nature of the person or knife) will be taken into custody, then, assuming that the police personnel abide by these policies, their action not to arrest a person with a small amount of marijuana or their act of taking into custody a knife-carrying student will be bias-free.

In contrast, the potential risk of bias manifesting in *highly discretionary* activities might be inferred from the experience of a municipal agency that was aggressive in its use of field interrogation cards. The agency leaders directed their personnel to engage in frequent consensual encounters and to collect and record information such as the person's name and location. The line personnel were told that this information could be valuable in preventing and solving crimes in the relevant areas, but they were given no formal guidance as to whom to engage for this purpose and under what circumstances. Some community members were very critical of this practice and accused the agency of targeting people of color, particularly, Blacks for these frequent encounters; and, indeed data showed that Blacks were disproportionately represented among the stops made by police. Asked in this context what direction the agency gave personnel about whom to stop, the response from agency leadership was, "we certainly don't tell them to target Blacks." The science implies, however, that, *barring any direction to the contrary,* officers told to engage in some high-discretion activity geared toward preventing or solving crimes will default to the group(s) they most link to crime and violence. In most humans, this will be males of color between 18 and 25.[19] This requires no animus towards those groups; it does not require conscious intention to target those groups. It requires only a human with the best of intentions—wanting to serve the community members by reducing crime in the area.

Bertrand et al. (2005) describe two other conditions that might increase the risk of implicit bias activation in a situation: ambiguity (see also Gaertner and Dovidio 2000) and time pressures (see e.g., Macrae et al. 1998; Payne 2006). The concept of ambiguity was raised above, in the context of "filling in" with stereotypes individuals who are "ambiguous stimuli." Similarly, implicit biases are activated when a person is facing ambiguous situations, and police face *many* ambiguous situations as a part of their work.

An NYPD court case and a New York state report both reference the possibility of police being impacted by biases in ambiguous situations. The first example of the potential for bias in ambiguous situations comes from the August 12, 2013 opinion of District Court Judge Shira A. Scheindlin, who held that the stop and frisk practices of the New York City Police Department (NYPD) violated Constitutional rights (*Floyd vs. City of New York*). In reflecting on a key concern in the case—the targeting of racial/ethnic minorities—Judge Scheindlin wrote, "Unconscious bias could help explain the otherwise puzzling fact that NYPD officers check 'Furtive Movements' in 48 % of the stops of blacks and 45 % of the stops of Hispanics, but

---

[19]As an important reminder here: Even if stereotypes are based in part on fact, police err when they treat the individual as if s/he fits the stereotype.

only 40 % of the stops of whites. There is no evidence that black people's movements are objectively more furtive than the movements of white people" (p. 45).

The second example comes out of a 2010 report that was produced by the New York State Task Force on Police-on-Police shootings. One pattern that the task force found (for both New York State and the nation) is that the off-duty, plain clothed officers who are killed by friendly fire are disproportionately individuals of color. In discussing this finding, the task force writes (2010, p. 3):

> Our conclusion from the review is clear: inherent or unconscious racial bias plays a role in shoot/don't-shoot decisions made by officers of all races and ethnicities. The role may be small and subtle, measured during simulations only in milliseconds of action or hesitation, but the patterns … are clear and consistent.

How might the concepts of bias and ambiguity apply to these tragic friendly fire encounters? As above, the argument is that ambiguous situations are more likely to activate implicit biases; the converse then, is that *unambiguous situations* should be *less likely* to activate implicit biases. The Task Force authors described a number of these tragic incidents, including the large number that involved police of color as the victims. In many of these events, the situation had ambiguous elements that could have produced implicit biases. But let me argue the converse for one of them to highlight the role of ambiguity. Officer Omar Edwards was killed by fellow officers in Harlem in May of 2009. Edwards, an African American, was off-duty and in plain clothes when he started chasing down the person whom he had found leaning into the broken window of his (Edward's) parked car. Edwards had his service revolver out as he ran. A car with three plainclothes officers turned down a street and found the escaping car burglar running toward them, followed by this African American with his gun out. Officer Dunton stopped the car, exited, and took cover behind the passenger side door and yelled toward the person with a gun, "Police! Stop! Drop the gun. Drop the gun." Reportedly, Edwards turned toward the voices with his gun in his hand "with his elbow 'locked'" (NYS Task Force Report 2010, page 17). Dunton, facing a firearm that was pointed at him, fired his own weapon and killed Edwards.

Did Edwards' race impact this tragedy? Maybe, but the concept of ambiguity implies that, with an unambiguous, immediate threat, biases based on demographics might have no impact. The threat Dunton faced lacked ambiguity—a gun was pointing at him and his colleagues. Would Dunton have shot a White individual who had turned toward him with a weapon trained on him? Arguably yes.

Time pressures can increase the risk of implicit bias activation (Bertrand et al. 2005). Fast-moving events can be more prone to implicit biases and police are certainly exposed to these. And, indeed, the two factors—ambiguity and fast moving—can easily coexist. If an officer enters into an ambiguous situation that requires quick action, that means s/he cannot gather more information to understand the situation at hand. Similarly, in a quick-moving situation, the officer has less time to reflect on his/her first-impression interpretations of the situation and to make corrections. As will be discussed below, *having time* to reflect on the possibility of a bias-produced misinterpretation of a situation and deciding to override those biases, is helpful for producing bias-free behavior (Lambert et al. 2003; Payne 2001).

Reducing and Managing Biases

The bad news from the science, reported above, is that even well-intentioned individuals have biases that can impact their perceptions and behavior. The good news from the science on implicit bias is that individuals can reduce and manage their biases. Indeed, some mechanisms for effectively addressing our implicit biases are different from those that might be used to address explicit ones: According to Dovidio and Gaertner (1999, p. 101.): "Whereas the traditional form of prejudice may be reduced by direct educational and attitude-change techniques, contemporary forms may require alternative strategies oriented toward the individual or involving intergroup contact." The answer is *not* trying to suppress our biases. Some individuals might claim they are color blind or gender blind or whatever-blind; others may aspire to be so. But both this claim and aspiration are highly improbable and, in fact, attempts to repress our biases can have unintended negative effects (Blair et al. 2001; Galinsky and Moskowitz 2000; Macrae et al. 1994; Monteith et al. 1998; Payne et al. 2001).[20]

Interventions start with educating individuals on implicit biases. This knowledge can help a person recognize when his/her own implicit biases manifest. That is, even though implicit biases can activate *outside of conscious awareness*, once educated, a person can become *cognizant* of them. The point was made earlier that our implicit biases do not necessarily line up with our conscious beliefs. In individuals who, at the conscious level, reject biases, stereotypes and prejudice, this recognition of their own implicit biases can motivate them to implement various mechanisms that the science shows can be used to reduce and manage biases (see Kang et al. 2012; Bennett 2010; Hernandez et al. 2013; for an overview, see Staats 2013). According to Devine et al. (2012, p. 1268): "First, people must be aware of their biases and, second, they must be concerned about the consequences of their biases before they will be motivated to exert effort to eliminate them."

Reducing and managing are linked to the concepts of "activation" of biases and "application" of biases, respectively (Gilbert and Hixon 1991; Kawakami et al. 2000). To reduce biases means that we are reducing the *activation* of stereotypes and biases in our thinking. This is neither simple, quick, nor 100 % effective, because it took us a lifetime to develop our biases. So, to the extent that biases are not eliminated, the person can still *manage* them; that is s/he can recognize activation and ensure that the biases are not "*applied*" to behavior.

---

[20]Attempts to suppress stereotypes can actually make the stereotype more accessible (Galinsky and Moskowitz 2000).

Reducing Biases

As above, it took us a lifetime to develop and reinforce our biases and so it is not simple to undo them. But science has shown that biases are not fixed; they are malleable (see e.g., Blair et al. 2001; Dasgupta and Asgari 2004; Dasgupta and Greenwald 2001; Karpinski and Hilton 2001; Kawakami et al. 2000; Rudman et al. 2001). This fact opens the door to several mechanisms that can serve to reduce biases—that is thwart their *activation* (for reviews, see Blair 2002; Devine 2001; Paluck 2012; Paluck and Green 2009). Two key concepts are the "contact theory" and "exposure to counterstereotypes."

Contact Theory

Pursuant to the contact theory, an individual's biases can be reduced through positive contact with members of other groups (e.g., stereotyped groups, "out-groups"). In describing the contact theory Tausch and Hewstone (2010, p. 544) write, "The notion that contact between members of different groups can, under certain conditions, reduce prejudice is one of the most prominent ideas underlying approaches to improve intergroup relations." Allport (1954) was key in the formulation of the "contact theory" (sometimes referred to as the "contact hypotheses") and he specified "favorable conditions" for producing the desired outcome from contact with others. As above, the contact or interaction must be of a *positive nature* and, according to Allport, is most powerful when (1) the two parties are interacting with equal status; (2) the individuals have a common goal; (3) the interaction is cooperative, not competitive; and (4) the contact is externally supported (for instance, by authorities). These four conditions are not *essential* to the success of the contact theory, but rather are conditions that can facilitate its positive impact (Pettigrew and Tropp 2006).

There is considerable empirical support for the contact theory generally, and of the greater impact of it when the conditions are met (see e.g., Pettigrew and Tropp 2006, who conducted a meta-analysis of 515 studies on the contact theory). Peruche and Plant (2006) tested the power of the contact theory using 50 police officers as subjects. As part of a multi-faceted study examining implicit bias in their police subjects, the researchers measured each subject's level of Black-crime implicit bias using the "shoot, don't shoot" methodology (measuring errors) and also used a survey to assess the quantity and quality of the subject's interactions with Blacks—both on and off the job. The findings provided affirmation of the contact theory. The officers who reported more positive personal contact with Blacks manifested less racial bias in the "shoot, don't shoot" computer simulator. The implications for policing are several and will be discussed in Chap. 3 of this book.

Exposure to Counterstereotypes

Another mechanism for reducing the activation of stereotypes is "exposure to counterstereotypes." This concept is easy to assimilate. If a person has an association between a group and a negative stereotype, exposure to members of that group who reflect the *opposite* of that negative stereotype can reduce the strength of the bias. Thus, for instance, if a person believes that the long-term unemployed are lazy people who do not want to work, this stereotype will be weakened if the person is exposed to individuals who are experiencing long-term unemployment but working diligently every day to get a job. This mechanism has received significant empirical support (see e.g., Blair and Banaji 1996; Blair et al. 2001; Correll et al. 2007a; Dasgupta and Greenwald 2001; Dasgupta and Rivera 2008; Karpinski and Hilton 2001).[21] As one example, Dasgupta and Greenwald (2001) found that exposing subjects to admired Black and disliked White exemplars reduced implicit racial bias.

The concept of counterstereotypes has been linked to high quality use-of-force training. Several of the "shoot, don't shoot" studies (e.g., Correll et al. 2007b; Sadler et al. 2012 described above) found different results for their police subjects, compared to their nonpolice subjects, for one but not both of the outcome measures. Recall that Correll et al. (2007b) compared police subjects and nonpolice subjects and looked at both speed of decision-making and errors. For the speed outcome, both groups (police and nonpolice) evidenced bias; but when the researchers examined errors, they found that police were much less likely than their nonpolice counterparts to make errors and, importantly, their errors were much less likely to reflect bias. The study by Correll et al. (2007b) was summarized in an article in *The Police Chief*, wherein the authors (Correll and Keesee 2009) report:

> ...the officers in these studies did show pronounced racial bias in their reaction times. Even with extensive training and experience, police still seem to call stereotypes to mind when they see a black target on the computer screen; however, the officers were ultimately able to override those associations and respond in an unbiased fashion.

The authors suggested that high quality use-of-force training might have produced this result, and the potential value of use-of-force simulator training has been linked theoretically and empirically to the concept of counterstereotypes. In theory, use-of-force role play training (such as that provided with video-simulator, judgment training) wherein the trainees are exposed to counterstereotypes (for instance, an elderly White woman who turns out to be a threat) could serve to reduce manifestation of biases in those often split-second use-of-force decisions. Several studies have assessed this empirically. Plant et al. (2005) and Plant and Peruche (2005) used "shoot, don't shoot" methods with both police and nonpolice subjects

---

[21]While there is a large body of literature finding support for the effectiveness of counterstereotypes for reducing bias, there are also some recent studies that raise questions about effectiveness (see e.g., Lybarger and Monteith 2011; Schmidt and Nosek 2010). More research is needed to identify the circumstances in which exposure to counterstereotypes has, or does not have, an effect. (For more, see Staats et al. 2015.)

to see if repeated exposure to counterstereotypes would reduce the manifestation of bias. In their study with nonpolice subjects, they conducted baseline testing of bias with the "shoot, don't shoot" methods. Related to the counterstereotypes theory, the subjects saw pictures ("stimuli") that were consistent with stereotypes: a Black man with a gun or a White man without a gun; but they were just as likely to see counterstereotypes, such as a White man with a gun or a Black man without a gun. The researchers confirmed their hypothesis that repeated exposure to "shoot, don't shoot" stimuli that included counterstereotypes reduced the biased application of force and this impact persisted on retests 24 h later.[22] In essence, through this repeated exposure, the subjects learned that race was non-diagnostic of threat. The researchers report:

> ...extensive practice with the program where race of face was unrelated to possession of a weapon led to the inhibition of racial concepts. Because race was non-diagnostic and paying attention to race only impaired performance on the shoot/don't shoot task, extensive exposure to the program encouraged the inhibition of the participants' racial categories (p. 152).

Plant and Peruche (2005) using police professionals as participants similarly found that repeated exposure to a ("shoot, don't shoot"-like) program, where the race of the person in the scene was unrelated to the presence of weapon, eliminated officers' bias (at least in the context of the study) in their application of force.

The unanswered question that is raised by the research of Plant and Peruche is whether the effects of the "training" will last beyond 24 h. Blair et al. (2001), based on their own research, speculate about the potential long-term impact of such exposures. Their common sense suggestion is that a single exposure would likely not produce long-term gains, but that repeated exposures over time "ought to effect more stable and long-lasting changes" (p. 838).

Below, scenario-based judgment training will be visited again and linked to an additional psychology-of-bias concept—"controlled responses"—through the studies of Correll et al. (2007a, b) and James et al. (2013, 2014, 2016).

Stereotype-Disconfirming Information and Cultural Sensitivity Training

The section above reports that biases can be reduced when a person is exposed to counterstereotypes. What if the person is not exposed to a counterstereotypical

---

[22]Importantly, Correll et al. (2007b) confirmed that it was, in fact, the exposure to the opposite of the stereotype that produced this positive benefit (versus some other mechanism, such as practice). These researchers conducted a similarly study wherein in one group of subjects performed a counterstereotype version and another group of participants perform a "pro-stereotypic version"—where unarmed Whites and armed Blacks were overrepresented. Biased use of force was reduced in the subjects exposed to the counterstereotype version, but not with the group exposed to the pro-stereotypic version.

person or group, but rather exposed to *information* about the group that reflects counterstereotypes? The research indicates that exposure to counterstereotype *information* can reduce biases. According to Hall, Crisp and Suen: "…exposure to outgroup stereotype-disconfirming information related to outgroups and outgroup members can lead to a reduction in implicit prejudice" (2009, p. 245; see also Park et al. 2007; Stone and Moskowitz 2011).

This finding is directly linked to "cultural sensitivity" training that many agencies provide to their employees. The nature and quality of the courses using this label vary greatly, but the science indicates that the courses that share factual, stereotype-disconfirming information about groups can reduce biases and stereotypes.

Blurring the Lines and Perspective Taking

Two additional mechanisms overlap with the *contact theory* and *exposure to counterstereotypes* concepts. They are "blurring the lines" and "perspective taking." Regarding the first, processes/activities that help reduce the distinction between "we" and "they" can reduce both explicit and implicit biases. Or said another way, processes that facilitate "they" becoming part of "us" can reduce biases (Hall et al. 2009; Woodcock and Monteith 2012). According to Hall et al. (2009, p. 246): "Reducing the distinction between 'us' and 'them' means that 'they' cannot be evaluated less positively than 'us'." In their study, these researchers found that the subjects who engaged in a task that required them to list characteristics that were common to both the ingroup and outgroup, manifested less implicit bias against the outgroup than their control group counterparts.

"Perspective taking" can also reduce biases (Galinsky and Moskowitz 2000). As reported by Staats (2014, p. 21), "taking the perspective of others has shown promise as a debiasing strategy, because considering contrasting viewpoints and recognizing multiple perspectives can reduce automatic biases." According to researchers, perspective taking "inspires empathy arousal" (Vescio et al. 2003, p. 456). For instance, Vescio et al. (2003) found that subjects who were encouraged to adopt the perspective of an African American who spoke about the challenges he faced by being part of a negatively stereotyped group reported more favorable attitudes toward African Americans. Similarly, Shih et al. (2013) demonstrated that perspective taking and empathy reduced implicit biases against Asian Americans.

Both of these concepts—blurring the lines and perspective taking—can be linked to the contact theory and exposure to counterstereotypes. Regarding contact theory, having positive contact can reduce the extent to which a person differentiates him/herself from others; getting to know people who are different from ourselves in a positive interaction can help us understand that we are more similar than different (blurring the lines). According to Hall et al., "… reduced differentiation is the key cognitive component of contact strategies" (2009, p. 250).

Similarly, the positive interactions may produce opportunities for perspective taking which would enhance the power of the contact to reduce biases.

Managing Biases Through Self-regulation

The processes described above can be used to reduce the *activation* of a stereotype or bias. No one imagines, however, that we can totally rid ourselves of our biases, so it is important that there is another mechanism to impact the *application* of stereotypes to behavior. If we recognize our implicit biases and are motivated to be fair and impartial, we can "self regulate" (Monteith 1993; Monteith et al. 2002; Monteith et al. 2010); we can choose to override our biases and implement bias-free behavior. The social scientists refer to these bias-free behaviors as "controlled responses" or "controlled processes" (Devine 1989).

Self-regulation is based on three components: (1) awareness, (2) motivation, and (3) controlling behavior (see Devine 1989; Devine et al. 2012). Above, I discussed the importance of awareness—that is, awareness of our implicit biases—and how it can produce motivation in people who want to be fair and impartial. Managing or regulating our biases—if we are aware and motivated—is as simple as choosing to implement bias-free behavior. If we are unaware of our biases or unconcerned about them, the default behavior will be biased. But, according to Devine, a motivated individual can displace those default biased behaviors with behaviors that are bias-free; a strong body of research indicates that motivated individuals can "exert control over their prejudiced responses" (Devine et al. 1991; Monteith et al. 2010; Monteith 1993; Monteith 1996; Monteith et al. 1993; Monteith et al. 1998).

There are, however, threats to our ability to manage biases (see review in Staats 2013). As previewed above, time pressures can thwart efforts at control (see Bertrand et al. 2005; Correll et al. 2007b; Payne 2006) as can "cognitive busyness" (see e.g., Correll et al. 2015). Both of these have great relevance to policing decisions. Regarding the cognitive busyness, Gilbert and Hixon (1991) found that, when individuals are facing "multiple demands, complex tasks, time pressures" (Reskin 2005, p. 34), there is an increased chance that they will act on an activated stereotype.[23]

The time factor is relevant to a study discussed above that was conducted by Correll et al. (2007b), which put both police subjects and nonpolice subjects through the "shoot, don't shoot" methods. This study provided good news regarding the benefits of high quality use-of-force training, but also how implementing controlled responses can take some time—even if only a fraction of a second. Recall, that the results regarding *speed of decision-making* evidenced

---

[23]Gilbert and Hixon (1991) reported that the cognitive busyness made it less likely that a stereotype would activate, but more likely, if activated, to produce a biased response.

"robust racial bias" on the part of both police and nonpolice subjects. The officer subjects were slower to act when the race and armed status were inconsistent with stereotypes (e.g., they faced an unarmed Black or an armed White). But, importantly, in terms of *errors* (shooting the unarmed person or not shooting the armed person), the police subjects were much less likely to manifest bias in their actions compared to the nonpolice subjects. From these results, Correll and his colleagues suggested that the combined results regarding speed and errors indicated that the officers were taking time (even if just a split-second) to implement *controlled responses* to thwart their natural biases (see Correll et al. 2014; Sim et al. 2013).

Fatigue may also reduce a person's ability to implement controlled responses, although the research is mixed. Two studies (Govorun and Payne 2006; Ma et al. 2013) showed that fatigue increased the manifestation of bias in weapon recognition and "shoot, don't shoot" studies, but James et al. (2015) showed no impact of fatigue on subject's performance on the IAT or in shooting simulation tasks.

Some very interesting and concerning research indicates that these police "controlled responses" can go too far—potentially putting officers in danger. Lois James, in her dissertation research (subsequently published in James et al. 2013, 2014) and subsequent research (James et al. 2016), examined implicit biases linking race/ethnicity to threat using more advanced "shoot, don't shoot" methods. Previous researchers had shown research subjects still photos portraying individuals with weapons or neutral objects in their hands or superimposed on their heads, and required the subjects to very quickly indicate by pressing keys whether the person was a threat ("shoot") or not a threat ("don't shoot"). Advancing these methods, James and colleagues developed scenarios like those used in police video training— wherein the officer "interacts" with an unfolding situation and ultimately has to decide whether the person in the scene is a threat or not, requiring force or not. The scenarios were developed to capture the complexity and tension of force encounters. Subject race varied in the scenarios—using Black, White or Hispanic individuals; all other variables were controlled so that the researchers could determine whether and how subject race/ethnicity impacted on the officers' decisions to shoot. As with the more traditional "shoot, don't shoot" studies, the study participants were supposed to shoot the people in the videos who posed a danger and not shoot those who were not. Outcome measures were errors and reaction time and the study participants included police officers.

The biases that James found in her police subjects were *opposite* of those found in prior studies. The police participants took *longer* to shoot Black subjects compared to Hispanic and White subjects and were less likely to shoot unarmed Black individuals than unarmed White or Hispanic individuals. In fact, officers were slightly more than three times less likely to shoot an unarmed Black person than an unarmed White person (James et al. 2016; see also Cox et al. 2014).

James et al. (2016) did not argue that the Black-crime implicit bias did not exist in these police subjects and in fact, a component of the research included a confirmation of a Black-crime implicit bias in the subjects. Instead, the researchers suggested several possibilities that are consistent with the implementation of controlled responses. James et al., conjectured that, because of the controversy surrounding the disproportionate shooting of Blacks, the study participants, although not told that racial bias was being studied, may have made an effort to be unbiased. Another possibility, the one they thought the most likely, is that the subjects manifested a "behavioral 'counter-bias' due to real-world concern over discipline, liability, or public disapproval" (p. 206). According to James et al, "This behavioral 'counter-bias' might be rooted in people's concerns about the social and legal consequences of shooting a member of a historically oppressed racial or ethnic group" (2014, p. 336). These studies were conducted *before* the events in Ferguson in 2014 reignited the national debate over race and police use of force, however even before August 2014 many officers may have been concerned about the consequences of using force, especially deadly force, against a Black person. They might have been concerned about departmental sanctions, prosecution, media attention, or even the safety of their families.[24] The consequences of a counter-bias phenomenon could be great. It may be that the controversy surrounding police racial bias could lead officers to hesitate when dealing with racial/ethnic minority subjects and put their own lives—or the lives of others—in danger.

James and I (James et al. 2016) summarize the three lines of research that identify factors that might impact officers' split-second decisions to shoot: (1) their human race-crime implicit biases, (2) the nature and quality of their use-of-force training, and (3) "counter bias" that might be precipitated by concerns about the consequences of using force against a racial/ethnic minority. As we explain (2016): "The strength of each of these forces will vary across officers, jurisdictions, and time periods—depending on personal characteristics, the nature and frequency of training, and the local and national (socio-political atmosphere)." The policy and training implications for these three lines of study are discussed elsewhere in this book.

Conclusion

The bad news from the science is that even well-intentioned individuals have biases that can impact their perceptions and behavior—producing discriminatory behavior. The good news from the science is that individuals, once educated on the science of implicit bias, can impact those biases. As above, individuals can both reduce and manage their biases—that is, they can impact the *activation* of the biases, and when that does not fully work, they can still negate the *application* of their biases to behaviors. Motivation was introduced as a key concept. Knowledge of our biases can induce motivated individuals to utilize the mechanisms described in this section. But even unmotivated individuals can be impacted by these processes. That is, there are ways that law enforcement agency leaders could harness these

---

[24]Evidence of this concern on the part of officers can be found among the anecdotes in David Klinger's 2004 book, *The Kill Zone: A Cop's Eye View of Deadly Force.*

mechanisms and impact even unmotivated individuals. They could manage their personnel in such a way as to enhance positive contact with diverse groups, blur the lines, expose their officers to stereotype disconfirming information, and enhance perspective taking. For instance, as discussed more fully below, an agency could implement street strategies wherein officers—motivated or otherwise—have positive contact with diverse individuals—reducing biases. But the greatest power of these mechanisms is in the context of individuals who *want* to be fair and impartial. Because of that limitation, we cannot rely on individual patrol officers and first-line supervisors within police agencies to ensure agency-wide fair and impartial policing on the streets of the jurisdiction. That is, we are not done if we raise consciousness and give motivated officers tools to be fair and impartial. More is required. We need agency leaders to implement various strategies that promote bias-free policing. Chapter 3 provides agency leaders with the tools they need to promote fair and impartial policing—based on the science of bias.

Chapter 3
A Comprehensive Program to Produce Fair and Impartial Policing

The science of bias helps to develop guidance for agency leaders who seek to promote fair and impartial policing. Reflecting the new paradigm, the agency must consider both the traditional target group—officers with explicit biases—and the "new" target group—the well-intentioned officers with implicit bias. These efforts can and should focus broadly on the various bases upon which people might be treated differently, including race, ethnicity, socioeconomic status, age, gender, gender identity, ability to speak English, sexual orientation, immigration status, and so forth. The Comprehensive Program, which is outlined in this chapter, is summarized as follows:

- The leadership of the agency conveys a commitment to fair and impartial policing.
- An agency has a meaningful policy that tells officers when they can and cannot use demographics and other factors to make law enforcement decisions.
- An agency attempts to recruit, hire, and promote diverse personnel and people who can police in an unbiased fashion.
- The agency implements policies that will help to reduce or eliminate the implicit biases that might manifest in the hiring, promotion, and evaluation processes.
- An agency has effective academy and in-service training directed to the ways that bias might manifest in even the best officers in the best departments.
- An agency directs and trains supervisors to promote bias-free policing.
- An agency maximizes the use of accountability mechanisms to promote bias-free policing.
- An agency makes an informed decision regarding whether and what system of measurement will be a part of its Comprehensive Program.
- An agency engages in ongoing efforts to strengthen the relationships between the department and the diverse communities that it serves.
- An agency adopts operations that support fair and impartial policing and the perceptions of it.

The sections below provide guidance for agencies consistent with the list above.

© The Author(s) 2017
L.A. Fridell, *Producing Bias-Free Policing*,
SpringerBriefs in Translational Criminology, DOI 10.1007/978-3-319-33175-1_3

The Leadership Message

The leader of an agency must convey his/her commitment to fair and impartial policing. His/her message will be heard by both personnel and community members and it takes a careful, nuanced communication to earn the trust of the community without making the personnel in the agency feel like they have been thrown under the bus. The savvy executive will be aware of how a message in the vein of "we have no biased policing" will be received by community members who think otherwise. I expect no such statement has ever changed the mind of a community member who believes that biased policing exists and, instead, such a message will likely increase frustration or even anger. (And as society becomes more familiar with the concept of implicit bias, this statement will increasingly be recognized as ignorant.) But the community stakeholders need to be aware of how a statement in the vein of, "we *have* biased policing" will be received by the police personnel. Personnel who have not yet been introduced to the "new paradigm" (that is, they haven't been introduced to the modern science perspective) will be offended or even angry. It will "feel" to them as if the leader just impugned their character—that s/he just announced that the department is comprised of individuals with explicit biases, such as racists. Producing this negative reaction on the part of personnel does not advance change efforts.

A nuanced message is required—particularly in the period of time before both the community and department are introduced to the new paradigm. It might take the form of this three-part message:

- Bias-free policing is required by the Constitution, essential to legitimate law enforcement, and promotes community trust and confidence.
- The members of this department are committed to bias-free policing.
- To promote fair and impartial policing, we are doing the following…

The first statement conveys an understanding of the importance of bias-free policing. The second statement neither affirms nor denies the existence of biased policing and, including "members of this department" conveys that it is not just the executive and his/her command staff members who are committed to bias-free policing, but so too are the rest of the personnel. Fair and impartial policing is not being done *to them*; it is being done *by them*.

Although the second statement does not affirm or deny the problem, the third sentence, although very positive, conveys the reality of its existence. Stating that the department is taking steps to produce fair and impartial implies that bias-free policing requires proactive efforts. The end of the third statement can be filled in with all of the relevant areas of the comprehensive response covered below. For instance, "To promote fair and impartial policing we have a policy defining and prohibiting biased policing, we seek to hire personnel who represent the diversity of the community and people who can police in an unbiased fashion, we are conducting top-to-bottom state-of-the art training …" and so forth.

So when and how do agency leaders convey this message? Of course, it is desirable to share this message *before* a biased policing crisis hits the agency—when the leader is on the defensive. Instead, it is best to be sharing this information in times of calm. For instance, this message could be conveyed:

- At the time that the agency implements new science-based training or adopts a new policy
- In an annual report with a new section entitled "Bias-Free Policing"
- At community meetings. This could be conveyed by the top leadership or by the first-line supervisors or mid-level leaders who meet regularly with community groups.[1]

The leader can also convey commitment to fair and impartial policing through the agency's mission statement, evaluations, activity reports, awards, and so forth. Toronto already had the following core values as part of its mission statement: honesty, integrity, respect, reliability, team work, fairness and positive attitude; it added "bias-free" to this list. Personnel evaluations communicate to the patrol officer and to his/her supervisor-evaluator what is important to the agency. Criteria for officer evaluation might include "ability to perform in a fair and impartial manner" or "performs in a manner that builds community trust and confidence in the agency." Supervisors could be evaluated on their attentiveness to, and handling of, biased policing concerns. (Granted, these are not easy to measure in an objective fashion, but that is probably true for other aspects of the evaluation as well.) In Kalamazoo, to emphasize the importance of trust building, the sergeants' regular reports on unit activity include not just arrests and other enforcement actions, but sections on "community interaction" and "building trust." An agency's award program might similarly recognize these valued behaviors. The Los Angeles Police Department (LAPD) awards, not just bravery, valor, and lifesaving, but also gives awards for distinguished service, community policing, and human relations.

But the real "message" from the leadership will come in the form of *action*, not words or even awards. The actions to promote fair and impartial policing are outlined in the remaining sections below.

Agency Policy

Most agencies have stand-alone policies on "biased policing," "racial profiling," or "bias-based policing." Most of these were originally adopted in the late 1990s and early 2000s; prior to that, agencies were more likely to have broad statements in their standard operating procedure about equal protection. A key aspect of these policies is the clear articulation regarding when the consideration of race/ethnicity

---

[1]Students in the Fair and Impartial Policing first-line supervisor course receive instruction on how to discuss biased policing in these community meetings.

and other demographics is *inappropriate* in carrying out duties and when it is legitimate ("information-led") policing to consider them. Indeed, it is important for agencies to *tell their employees* when it is and is not appropriate to use demographics to make their law enforcement decisions. According to Fridell and Scott (2005, p. 316): "Executives shouldn't assume that all of their personnel use race/ethnicity the same way and should be concerned that their use may be broader than what the executive believes is just."

Developing this communication requires that the agency define biased policing. A conceptual definition of biased policing is the "inappropriate use of race/ethnicity or other demographics in deciding with whom or how to intervene." There is no consensus around the key term in that definition, "inappropriate." There are differences of opinions (legal and otherwise) and the United States Supreme Court has not weighed into provide nationwide guidance (outside of cases involving illegal immigration along the U.S. border).[2] Having a meaningful policy may not impact officers with explicit biases, as they may be unconcerned about their prejudices and determined to act on them, even if contrary to agency policy. However, an executive has an obligation to communicate the parameters to all individuals in the agency. The science of bias tells us we are not blind to demographic characteristics, as much as we might want to be. If an agency educates its personnel on biases and asks them to manage them, it must also clearly state when it is appropriate to consider race, ethnicity, and other factors and when it is not.

Policy Models Defining Biased Policing

There are several policy models in use in North America. Some popular ones do not provide clear and reasonable guidance to personnel; some are quite bad. One example of the latter is the common "solely" policy model.[3] Although the wording may vary, the essence of such a policy is that officers are prohibited from using race, ethnicity, and so forth as the "sole" basis for making a decision (such as a decision to arrest, a decision to request consent to search). This definition is wholly inadvisable because it defines the problem of biased policing right out of existence; it defines a very narrow swath of decisions that are prohibited. First of all, it references the very rare circumstance when police make a decision based on a single factor; most decisions by police are based on a confluence of factors, not on a single factor. But pursuant to a "solely" policy, an officer is only violating the

---

[2]See Carbado and Harris (2011) for an overview of the US Supreme Court cases on the use of race. Because there are some lower court decisions regarding the acceptable use of race, ethnicity and other factors, agencies should assess relevant case law before adopting a policy. A review of statutory definitions is contained in NAACP (2014).

[3]The Commission on Accreditation for Law Enforcement Agencies (CALEA) can be credited with early adoption of a standard for "biased-based profiling." As of this writing, CALEA is revisiting this standard and removing the "solely" language from it.

policy when she makes a decision based on a single factor and that factor is race or ethnicity (or another demographics listed in the policy). A hypothetical helps to highlight the weakness of this policy model. Consider an officer who is monitoring a controlled intersection. Many people run the stop sign, but this officer only tickets young, Hispanic males *because they are young, Hispanic males* for their violations and lets everyone else go ticket-free. Most people would consider this biased policing, but this officer has not violated a "solely" policy. He did not make his decision based on a single factor, such as race; he made his decision to ticket based on age, gender, and race (and arguably, age, gender, race, *and the traffic violation*). It appears that "solely" policies are still the most common.[4] Many of them were adopted in the late 1990s or early 2000s when agency leaders had little guidance and few models existed for their consideration.

Our conceptual framework for thinking about more reasonable limits on the use of demographics for police work starts with the following concept: *We must treat all demographic groups the same unless there is a legitimate reason not to.* So that concept then begs the question: *When, in the context of police decision-making, is it legitimate NOT TO treat members of all demographic groups the same?* The answer is: *when there is actionable intelligence that justifies differential treatment.* There are two policy models that reflect different interpretations of when information is actionable intelligence that justifies differential treatment. I will refer to these as the "first circle" and "second circle" policies because the second circle policy fully incorporates the definition of the first—but provides for broader uses beyond it. (Picture one circle inside another.) The first-circle policy, also referred to as the "suspect specific" model, is the narrower model in terms of the circumstances in which it is acceptable to use demographics for police decisions. This version reflects the universally accepted notion that, when police have a specific suspect description that includes race and ethnicity (or other demographics) as one component, the police can use the demographic information to guide their investigation/actions. As an example, if police receive information that a credible store owner reported that his store was just robbed by a 5'8" to 6' Asian wearing a red sweatshirt, blue jeans and red tennis shoes, the police in that area following the robbery would focus on individuals meeting that description. "Asian" would be a legitimate part of the confluence of factors that might guide their work.[5] Departments with a first-circle policy recognize the legitimate use of demographics in the context described above, but allow *no other use* of them in police decision-making. There are many policies that reflect the first-circle model, although their wording varies. An example of a first-circle definition is as follows:

---

[4]This is based on the author's (albeit unsystematic) review of policies around the nation.

[5]Not all suspect descriptions are equally valuable/valid. The stronger ones are provided by credible sources in a timely manner; and the more descriptors included (e.g., height, weight, clothes, race), the stronger it is. Sometimes a race-descriptor is not powerful in a context—for instance in a neighborhood that is populated primarily by the same race as that provided in the description.

Personnel[6] shall not consider actual or perceived race, ethnicity, national origin, gender, gender identity, sexual orientation, socioeconomic status, religion and/or age in carrying out their duties, except when seeking one or more specific individuals who have been identified or described in part by any of the above listed characteristics. In those circumstances, personnel may rely on these characteristics only in combination with other appropriate factors.

The second-circle model recognizes the legitimacy of using demographics associated with a specific suspect description (as articulated in the first-circle definition), but goes further in allowing the use of demographics for making police decisions. The extra "latitude" that it provides reflects a conceptual extension of the first-circle concept. It still limits the use of demographics to those situations where suspect descriptions provide intelligence, but it does not limit the use of demographics to only those situations wherein police have a full description of an individual. The following hypothetical helps to convey this point and to show the distinction between the first-circle policy and the second-circle version.

A number of middle school students have reported that adult, Hispanic men are selling fake IDs around a shopping mall. Officers have consistent, trustworthy descriptions that the perpetrators are adult, Hispanic, males, but they do not have sufficiently "full" and reliable individual suspect descriptions (e.g., individuals described with multiple factors such as ethnicity, gender, clothes, facial hair, height).

Under a first-circle policy, an officer investigating these crimes could not consider a person's ethnicity around the mall as even one factor in the confluence of factors that might guide his decision making (decision to engage in a consensual encounter, decision to detain). The second-circle policy would allow police who are investigating this scheme to consider "male" and "Hispanic" as part of the confluence of factors that might produce the basis, for example, of a detention or other intervention. Other parts of that "confluence" might include location in the mall, behavior consistent with the illegal scheme, and so forth.

The key relevant portion of a second-circle policy might read:

Personnel may not consider race, ethnicity, national origin, gender, gender identity, sexual orientation, socioeconomic status, religion, and/or age except when credible, timely intelligence relevant to the locality links a person or people of a specific race, ethnicity, national origin, gender, gender identity, sexual orientation, socioeconomic status, religion, and/or age to a specific unlawful incident, or to specific unlawful incidents, criminal patterns or schemes. In those circumstances, personnel may rely on these characteristics only in combination with other appropriate factors.[7]

---

[6]Using "personnel" rather than "officers" or "sworn personnel" indicates that the policy applies to all members of the agency, including civilians who might be staffing the front desk or handling 9-1-1 calls.

[7]This tracks closely to the policy that applies to federal agencies for "all activities other than routine or spontaneous law enforcement activities" (U.S. Department of Justice 2015). It reads (p. 2), "In conducting all activities other than routine or spontaneous law enforcement activities, Federal law enforcement may consider race, ethnicity, gender, national origin, religion, sexual orientation, or gender identity only to the extent that there is trustworthy information, relevant to the locality and time frame, that links persons possessing a particular listed characteristic to an

The key elements of this model are:

- *Locally relevant*: This element requires that the intelligence will be linked to a specific geographic area, such as a park, an intersection, or a neighborhood. For instance, Asians are stealing hub caps from the cars parked along such-and-such streets. This wording recognizes that the intelligence might be "relevant" to an area, even if it was not produced for that area specifically. For instance, recall that in the hours and days after the 9-11 attacks, we did not know as a country whether the attack was over. At that point, the fact that several terrorist events had just occurred and all of the participants were of Arab descent would have allowed local officials to use "Arab descent" in conjunction with other factors in making law enforcement decisions, such as decisions to detain.
- *Link between a demographic and a particular crime or crime category*: In the geographically relevant area, there is a demographic group that is linked to a particular crime (e.g., robbery) or category of crimes (drug-related crimes).[8]
- *Credible and timely intelligence*: The link referenced above is based on credible (not based on biases, rumor, a single report, etc.), timely (i.e., not stale) information/intelligence.
- *Adding the demographic to the confluence of factors*: The linkage above does not allow for police intervention with any person in that demographic group but rather, allows the officer to add the demographic variable to other factors (e.g., behavior, time of day) in making a duty-related decision. For instance, the demographic might become a part of the totality of circumstances that produces reasonable suspicion to detain.

Another example that fits with the second-circle parameters is as follows: In and around a particular two-block area of the city where the residents are primarily people of color, police know from recent undercover buys, informants, and prior arrests that the White students from the nearby college come into the area to buy drugs. The elements are present. In a particular geographic area (two-block area), the police have credible intelligence (based on undercover buys, informants, and prior arrests) that links a specific demographic group (young, White individuals) to a particular crime (drug buys). Pursuant to the second-circle model, the police could include "White" and "young" as elements of the confluence of factors that might

---

(Footnote 7 continued)

identified criminal incident, scheme, or organization, a threat to national or homeland security, a violation of Federal immigration law, or an authorized intelligence activity. In order to rely on a listed characteristic, law enforcement officers must also reasonably believe that the law enforcement, security, or intelligence activity to be undertaken is merited under the totality of the circumstances, such as any temporal exigency and the nature of any potential harm to be averted. This standard applies even when the use of a listed characteristic might otherwise be lawful."

[8]A conceptual extension of this policy goes beyond *criminals* who are linked to a demographic; it might be a *victim* group that has the demographic link to the crime (e.g., undocumented, Hispanic residents). Prevention efforts by police might be focused on a particular group based on this linkage.

provide the basis for an intervention. Other elements might include the time of day, behavior (e.g., slowing the car by known sales areas), and so forth.

Another example comes from a Canadian city. In a particular area of downtown, Roma women were robbing other women on the street of their jewelry. The police knew this from a number of victim reports that consistently described the perpetrators as Roma women.[9] In an agency with a suspect-specific policy, the officers could consider "Roma" and "female" as part of their efforts only if they had a full (multifactor) description of an individual or individuals that included these two factors. In an agency with a second-circle policy, the officers *could* consider Roma and female, along with other factors (e.g., location, time of day, behavior), based on these multiple, credible reports—even without those other single-person descriptors. They could, for instance, inform the public about the description of the perpetrators and attend, in their investigation and prevention efforts, to Roma women in the area whose behavior was suspect.

As above, reasonable minds will differ as to when it is acceptable to use demographics to make police decisions—that is, when demographics provide "actionable intelligence." Some police executives and community stakeholders will believe that the second-circle parameters are acceptable; others will believe that only the first-circle model sets reasonable parameters. There is an additional factor that executives and community stakeholders should consider when making a decision to adopt one model or the other. The suspect-specific model has a "bright line" that the second-circle model does not. The former policy is very straightforward; the outlines for the use of demographics are very clear. It would take about five minutes to train, including the provision of examples. The second-circle policy, on the other hand, does not have this bright line. In fact, all of its components, if not kept "tight" through training and supervision, have the potential for a slippery slope into biased policing. For instance, what is "locally relevant?" In concept, this is supposed to mean that the intelligence-based association between a demographic and criminal activity is directly linked to a geographically circumscribed area, such as a two-block area, intersection, park, and so forth. But, this could slip into "all parks in the jurisdiction," "two adjacent neighborhoods," the "north side of the city," and the "city overall." There are no set parameters on "locally" and so this is one source of a slippery slope.

And what volume and source of information provides an acceptably strong link between a demographic and a particular crime or category of crimes? Can the information be from four reports, or must it be from 30? Must 90 % of our known perpetrators of this crime match this demographic or is 51 % acceptable? Can the information come from prior arrests, which themselves might reflect the biased focus of police on one group? Because there are no easy answers to these questions, the volume/source parameter, too, has a slippery slope.

---

[9]This pattern became a part of the discussion of the agency in deciding whether to adopt a first-circle or second-circle model. If the officers could not consider "Roma women," did that also mean that they could not describe the perpetrator characteristics to the public as part of a prevention effort?

Because there is no "bright line," the second-circle policy should only be adopted by agencies that are willing to effectively train and supervise its use. A community with an agency that is not known for its ability to train well and hold its personnel to account would not be well served by a second-circle policy.

Anyone arguing for parameters set beyond the second-circle model is on tenuous ground; any other uses of demographics to make law enforcement decisions is, arguably, not "actionable intelligence." An individual or agency might be tempted, for instance, to consider demographics when that demographic is disproportionately involved in criminal activity (without the specific delimiting parameters imposed by the second-circle policy). Few in policing would actually make the argument that this is acceptable, but without clear constraints set by policy, some well-meaning humans with normal biases will default to this usage. This usage runs counter to an argument presented earlier that, even if certain demographic groups are disproportionately represented among people who commit crime, police are not justified in treating the individuals as if they represent that stereotype or generalization. Doing so is unsafe, ineffective and unjust.[10]

Another use of demographics outside of the two model policies, is articulated by some in law enforcement; some will even argue vehemently on its behalf. They will argue that law enforcement must consider race when, for instance, a White person is in a mostly Black area or a Black person is in a mostly White area. (Some will make similar arguments about the beat-up car in the high-income area, or the expensive car in the low-income area.) This usage of demographics reflects training that police received just a few decades back, but, I believe, provides no actionable intelligence that would allow an officer to treat a Black person on a "White" street different from a White person on that same street, or vice versa. It implies that there are some people in this country who "do not belong" in some areas. Any police leader arguing for a policy that would allow for these "race out of place stops" should be required to put that provision in writing and be willing to stand up in front of the county or city council and propose that wording, which would probably read: "An officer may use race and ethnicity in his/her decision making if a person's demographic does not fit the demographics of the area." Since such a provision in a policy will likely raise more than just the eyebrows of concerned community members (it will likely raise ire), an agency might instead follow the lead of Tampa PD, the policy of which (SB 536) included a specific statement declaring "race out of place" stops to be biased policing. Such an add-on to a policy might read:

> It is biased policing if an officer's decisions/actions are based on the fact that the individual's demographics (e.g., race, income) are different from the demographics of the majority of the residents in the area in which the individual is found.

---

[10]It is important to note here, that in some circumstances "disproportionately represented" could be legitimately used to meet one of the requirements of the second circle policy. Recall, one element is a "Link between a demographic and a particular crime or crime category" (based on credible, timely intelligence). This is, however, only one element of the second circle policy, and this link between a demographic and a crime must be specific to a circumscribed geographic area and only considered along with other factors (such as behavior and time of day).

The discussion above regarding first-circle and second-circle models is about an agency conveying to personnel when it is appropriate to use demographic and other factors to make decisions and when it is not. It is the critical element of a policy. Other policy considerations are discussed below.

Other Policy Considerations

In developing policy, departments must also think about:

- The title of the policy
- What demographics or other characteristics to list as prohibited factors
- To what police decision/actions the proscription against biased policing should apply
- Enforcement language
- Staying focused
- Conveying the policy content to personnel.

Each of these is discussed below.

Title

Policies use various phrases in their titles—"racial profiling," "bias-based profiling," "biased policing." Some agencies are adopting more positive language such as "Impartial Policing" or "Bias-Free Policing"; such language reflects the agency's aspiration and might be less offensive to personnel. But agencies need to think about the perspective of concerned community members, not just personnel, in deciding upon their terminology. For instance, some community members may believe that the "impartial policing" wording is putting too positive a "spin" on a serious issue. Some might even advocate for maintenance of the traditional term, "racial profiling." For instance, when the PD of the San Francisco area Bay Area Rapid Transit (BART) conferred with its Citizen Review Board about the agency's policy title and content, the leadership and Independent Police Auditor learned that some members did not want the agency to abandon the "racial profiling" terminology. The Independent Police Auditor, in a memo dated 2/10/2014 wrote: "As expressed by members of the BART Citizen Review Board at its January 13, 2014 regular meeting … there is good cause to refrain from simply abandoning the term 'racial profiling' altogether in the title and body of this policy. The continued inclusion of that term may prove to be of substantial assistance to individuals who are already familiar with it and are seeking to initiate a complaint of misconduct on that basis." The BART PD adopted the policy title: "Racial profiling or bias-based policing."

List of Demographics

There is not one, correct list of demographics that might be included in a biased policing policy (and, in fact, the list might depend in part on the demographics of the jurisdiction). It is positive that, since the early 2000s, agencies have moved beyond the traditional "short list," that included race, ethnicity and maybe national origin, but we want to guard against a list of demographics getting ridiculously long. Conceptually, the list should include factors that are most likely to produce biased behavior on the part of humans, including police. High priority factors to consider are: race, ethnicity, national origin, gender, gender identity, sexual orientation, religion, and socioeconomic status. Some of the additional factors listed by agencies include physical or mental disability, marital status, fraternal affiliation, dress, age, and cultural group.[11]

Behaviors/Actions Encompassed

A policy will designate which police behaviors/actions are encompassed by its restriction on the use of demographics and it should reference virtually all job-related actions. Unfortunately, many policies only apply the limits on the use of demographic characteristics to a subset of job-related decisions/actions. Those policies might limit the reach to only fourth amendment intrusions by limiting the use of demographics to "develop reasonable suspicion or probable cause." A policy with this narrow application of the limits (in the use of demographics) to only fourth amendment actions, would, by omission, *allow* an officer to freely use demographics as factors in decisions regarding from whom to request consent to search, consensual encounters, whom to treat with respect, whom to give a ticket versus a warning. This is unacceptable. Some policies list only what, for many years, were the (minimally) required CALEA actions, which are traffic contacts, field contacts, and asset seizure and forfeiture efforts.[12] Wording that reflects a narrow application (of the limits on the use of demographics) to fourth amendment actions is as follows: "Except as provided below, personnel shall not consider race, ethnicity, [etc.] in establishing either reasonable suspicion or probable cause to include but not be limited to traffic contacts, field contacts, and asset forfeiture efforts." [The provision "provided below" would set forth first-circle or second-circle parameters.] In contrast to this narrow application, the wording in a policy should be such that all actions/decisions are encompassed (including, for instance, consensual encounters,

---

[11]Some agencies include an additional "catch-all, such as "any other identifiable group"; this is arguably overly broad and inadvisable. For instance, would the inclusion of "any other identifiable group" preclude police consideration of gang affiliation?

[12]As above, as of this writing, CALEA is revising its standard on this topic; the new draft wording refers to "all police actions".

victim services, requests for consent to search). The following italicized words help to convey this point: "Except as provided below, personnel shall not consider race, ethnicity, [etc.] in *carrying out their duties.*"[13]

An add-on to this broad application to all law enforcement decisions could read: *This restriction on the use of these factors does not apply to agency activities designed to strengthen the department's relationship with its diverse communities.* This allows for the "targeting" of outreach activities to, for instance, Somalis; young, Hispanic males; the transgender community; undocumented immigrants; and so forth.

Enforcement Provisions

Policy should reference the role of supervisors and state how the agency will handle situations when biased actions are suspected. For instance, the Fayetteville PD policy indicates that:

- Supervisors will ensure that all personnel under their command are familiar with the content of this policy and are operating in compliance
- Supervisors are responsible for being alert to any language or conduct indicating bias ...

A statement should indicate that, "Violations of this policy shall result in training, counseling, discipline, or other remedial intervention as appropriate to the violation." Because bias might be unintentional, it is important that the list of possible interventions include informal and non-punitive responses such as training and counseling. Similarly, the agency should not *require* that a concern about biased actions be processed through the formal complaint review entity. Instead, the agency should allow for informal resolution through the chain of command. As discussed further below, concerns about bias (for instance, on the part of a supervisor) may be based on evidence that is below the level of proof required to sustain a complaint (and otherwise inappropriate for formal complaint review). The policy should leave open the option of informal intervention; otherwise, behavior that *should* be addressed might be ignored altogether.

CALEA Provisions: To meet the requirements of the Commission on Accreditation for Law Enforcement Agencies (CALEA), the policy must additionally reference training to include legal aspects and an "annual administrative review of agency practices including citizen concerns."

---

[13]Another way to produce this broad application is to take out reference to specific activities altogether. Thus, for instance, a policy might read: "Except as provided below, personnel shall not consider race, ethnicity, [etc.]." By not referencing acts or decisions, the implication is that the policy applies to all of them, which is desirable.

Staying Focused

An example of a second-circle policy is contained in Fig. 3.1. The first-circle version would differ only in the contents of the second paragraph under "Policy." As can be seen in this figure, these policies need not be long, and in fact being short and to the point might aid officer recall and ensure that the key elements do not get

---

Bias-Free Policing
("Second Circle" Model)

[Meets CALEA Requirements (1.2.9)]

I. **PURPOSE**

Biased policing undermines legitimate law enforcement efforts, alienates community members and fosters community distrust. This policy is intended to reaffirm this department's commitment to bias-free policing, to clarify the circumstances in which agency personnel can consider race, ethnicity, national origin, gender, gender identity, sexual orientation, socio-economic status, religion, disability, and/or age when carrying out duties.

II. **DEFINITIONS**

Biased Policing: The inappropriate consideration of specified characteristics in carrying out duties.

Specified Characteristics: Race, ethnicity, national origin, gender, gender identity, sexual orientation, socio-economic status, religion, disability, and/or age when making law enforcement decisions.

III. **POLICY**

It is the policy of this department to provide law enforcement services and to enforce the law equally, fairly and without discrimination toward any individual or group.*

Agency personnel may not consider the specified characteristics except when credible, timely intelligence relevant to the locality links a person or people of a specified characteristic to a specific unlawful incident, or to specific unlawful incidents, criminal patterns or schemes. In those circumstances, personnel may rely on these specified characteristics only in combination with other appropriate factors.

It is biased policing if an officer's decisions/actions are based on the fact that the individual's demographics (e.g., race, income) are different from the demographics of the majority of the residents in the area in which the individual is found.

These restrictions on the use of these specified characteristics do not apply to law enforcement activities designed to strengthen the department's relationship with its diverse communities.

Fig. 3.1 Example of a second-circle policy

<u>IV.</u>   **TRAINING AND COMPLIANCE**

    A. Personnel shall receive training in bias-free policing, including the legal and psychological aspects of it.

    B. Every member of this department shall perform his/her duties in a bias-free manner and is responsible for promptly reporting any known instances of biased policing to a supervisor.* Also, where appropriate, officers are encouraged to intervene at the time the biased policing incident occurs.**

    C. Supervisors shall ensure that all personnel in their command are familiar with the content of this policy and will be alert and respond to indications that biased policing is occurring.

    D. Violations of this policy shall result in training, counseling, discipline or other remedial intervention as appropriate to the violation.

    E. There shall be an annual administrative review of agency practices including citizen concerns.

*Denotes wording taken from, or paraphrased based on, Lexipol's Policy 401.
**Denotes wording taken from the IACP Model Policy "Unbiased Policing" (2015).

Fig. 3.1 (continued)

lost in other, extraneous content. Unfortunately, it is fairly common to see reiterated in an agency's biased policing policy, other policy provisions that are also contained elsewhere in the standard operating procedures. This might include the definitions for search, reasonable suspicion, and/or probable cause; procedures for professional traffic stops or consent searches; and so forth. While well-intentioned (and I expect some policy-writers think that a longer policy will look better to concerned community members), filling the biased policing policy with extraneous material is not helpful.

Personnel Knowledge of Policy Content

Standard operating procedures are so lengthy and detailed that it is understandable (although unfortunate) that personnel do not know all of its contents. The content of an agency's biased policing policy, however, should be a priority in terms of knowledge and understanding on the part of personnel. It should be trained as frequently as the agency trains its personnel on its use-of-force policy. In a northern city, it became clear to me through the process of training in Fair and Impartial Policing that the practice on the streets in terms of using demographics to make law enforcement decisions did not match the written policy. The policy in the books reflected a first-circle model, the behavior on the street reflected the broader second-circle parameters. An agency that takes seriously its commitment bias-free policing will have a clear, well-written policy and, *further*, make sure that personnel know of its content and the agency's expectations that they will adhere to it.

Recruitment, Hiring, and Promotions

Promoting fair and impartial policing and the perceptions of it through recruitment, hiring, and promotion breaks down into three objectives. The agency wants to:

- Recruit and hire individuals who represent the diversity of the community
- Hire people who can police in an unbiased fashion
- Guard against implicit biases in managerial decisions, such as hiring, promotion, and evaluations.

Each of these will be covered below.

Recruiting/Hiring Individuals Who Represent the Diversity of the Community

Recruiting and hiring diversity is not new to policing and so will not take up too much space here; existing resources provide strong guidance to agencies.[14] For decades, police departments across the nation have implemented efforts to increase the diversity on their forces. The "why's" for these efforts are as follows:

> Having a department that reflects the community it serves helps to build community trust and confidence, offers operational advantages, improves understanding and responsiveness, and reduces perceptions of bias (IACP 2007, p. 10).[15]

We do not target "minorities," however defined, because we think they will not have biases. Everyone has biases and, as reported in Chap. 2, people can even have biases against their own group. But bringing in underrepresented groups can impact the human biases of agency personnel through the contact theory. Having a diverse agency means that personnel will have positive contact with people who are different from themselves.

Most of the efforts to date have focused on increasing representativeness in terms of gender and race/ethnicity, although some agencies are also working to increase representation of various religious minorities (e.g., Muslims), specific nationalities/cultures (e.g., Hmong, Somali), and LGBT populations.

---

[14]See for instance, "Increasing Diversity in Police Departments" (Kasdan 2006); "Law Enforcement Recruitment Toolkit" (COPS Office/IACP Leadership Project 2009); "Increasing Organizational Diversity in 21st Century Policing: Lessons from the U.S. Military" (Haddad et al. 2012); "Identifying Barriers to Diversity in Law Enforcement Agencies" (Matthies et al. 2012); and "Community Centered Policing: A Force for Change" (West 2001). For a specific focus on LGBTQ communities, see *Gay and Lesbian Cops: Diversity and Effective Policing* (Colvin 2012) and *Best Practices in Policing and LGBTQ Communities in Ontario* (Ontario Association of Chiefs of Police 2013).

[15]See also "Why Have a Multicultural Workforce?" in Oliver (2014).

Resources providing guidance (see footnote #14) highlight the importance of:

- Making a full agency commitment to diversity, setting goals, and measuring progress
- Developing trust and confidence on the part of the diverse communities within the jurisdiction
- Tapping into internal knowledge, such as asking employees from underrepresented groups what drew them to policing or to the agency
- Using all officers as recruiters
- Making sure the entrance requirements are necessary
- Reaching out to prospects where they live, work, worship and play
- Partnering with minority-serving institutions/entities.

The Minneapolis Police Department (MPD) serves a very diverse city and has attempted to bring that diversity into the agency.[16] The recruitment team is comprised of diverse individuals, including women, gays/lesbians, people of color, and various nationalities (e.g., Somali). This team is beating the bushes for potential applications from underrepresented groups. According to Chief (ret) Dragom (2015):

> ... an agency cannot wait for the candidates to come to the department; the department needs to go to them. True recruitment means going outside the agency's comfort zone [and] meeting the candidates on their home turf. This is not only effective, but demonstrates the agency's devotion to getting diverse candidates and eventually diverse police officers in the department.

The MPD team members spend much of their time out in the various diverse communities talking about police work and handing out applications and brochures. For instance, in the Somali neighborhoods, they might visit the residential housing complex or walk into a coffee shop with department applications. They will hold a recruiting seminar at the local mosque and meet with the youths in the Big Brother and Big Sister program. They recruit Native Americans at the Native American Center and the schools that are magnet schools for Native Americans. They partner with local pastors who refer candidates to the department and place information about job opportunities in Church bulletins. The agency has extensive outreach to young people to engender positive views about police that might translate into interest in a law enforcement career. Also important to their recruitment efforts are their three "feeder programs" that MPD uses to target underrepresented groups: Police Explorers, Cadets, and Community Service Officers.

As above, a key objective for agencies is to bring in applications from a diverse population and then hire the individuals who will contribute to overall agency excellence. But even if an agency is successful in bringing in those diverse applications, its work is not done. It can be worthwhile to ensure that those applicants from underrepresented groups have every chance to succeed in meeting

---

[16]MPD sworn personnel are comprised of 14.8 % female and 21 % people of color. The residents of the city of Minneapolis are 24 % people of color.

the agency's high hiring standards. The first step is to determine if the agency is losing underrepresented groups during the multi-step screening process and, if it is, to determine whether it can stop or reduce this loss. One example comes from a coastal city in south Florida that was in dire need of Spanish-speaking officers. Bilingual Hispanics were applying, but they were washing out at the swim test. This fact was not known to the individuals in the agency who could intervene, until the agency conducted an assessment of its hiring process and the loss of underrepresented groups. Reasonable minds might differ on how to remedy this loss (e.g., get rid of the standard if it is not imperative, refer applicants to swimming lessons, train individuals to swim once hired), but the key was conducting the assessment of loss so that the agency could (and did) intervene to increase the likelihood that the Hispanics would succeed through the screening.

MPD systematically tracks applicants from key underrepresented groups through the steps of the screening process. The spreadsheet has columns that reflect gender and race/ethnicity categories and the rows are as follows:

- Applicants

  - Lacks minimum qualifications
  - Incomplete applications

- Provided proof of POST assessment
- Fitness assessment

  - Invited
  - Withdraw
  - No Show
  - Passed Fitness
  - Failed Fitness

- Oral Interview

  - Invited
  - Failed Oral
  - Passed Oral

- Backgrounds

  - Sent to backgrounds
  - Withdrew
  - Failed
  - Passed

- Conditional Job Offer

  - Declined

- Took Psychological Test

  - Not recommended
  - Recommended

- Took Medical Test
  - Passed
  - Failed

- Final Job Offer

With the spreadsheet, the agency can determine how well females and racial/ethnic minorities fare at each step, compared to the majority groups.

These data have led to various interventions to increase the success of diverse candidates. The first thing noticed by the MPD personnel was that many applicants —including, but not limited to, diverse applicants—did not submit the POST documentation that was required before the fitness test. For one round of hiring, this drop off represented almost 60 % of the applicants. Sending out a reminder email before the fitness test brought 66 % of the missing-docs-applicants back into the process, including women and candidates of color.[17]

MPD also took to heart the caution, "don't screen on what you can train" and applied it to the fitness test that had led to the disproportionate loss of women and people of color. Instead of producing a pass/fail outcome (with a "fail" resulting in a drop from hiring consideration), the agency switched to a fitness score from low to high. If a person did not pass one standard or even two (of the five), s/he was able to continue through the screening process, albeit with a lower performance score than his/her peers. If s/he turns out to be an otherwise strong potential hire, the agency brings the person up to physical fitness standards through training.

The Kalamazoo Police Department (KPD) also assesses loss of racial/ethnic minorities and females during the screening process. The KPD learned through the analysis that one underrepresented group was doing poorly on the math portion of the written test. Upon closer inspection KPD personnel determined that the members of the group were getting the answers right, but not completing the section in the time allotted for it. After conferring with the test developers, the department switched to an overall-test time limit, rather than time limits by section, and increased the pass rate of the group.

The LAPD has implemented many of the practices above and additionally, it gives the initial test at varied locations around the city and mentors applicants from traditionally underrepresented groups through the process.

As above, bringing in diversity is not a new objective for policing, and many more police departments could be highlighted here with innovative "best practices." But it is important to note that this should not be the sole job of the police department in a jurisdiction. If community members seek a more diverse force, then there needs to be a comprehensive and unified effort. Is the city council willing to raise starting salaries to compete more effectively with neighboring agencies? Are the African-American clergy willing to identify prospective hires and invite police

---

[17]The agency *did* consider the fact that neglecting to send in the form on time might reflect lack of attention to detail or lack of follow-through, but personnel decided that this one transgression was not worth eliminating a candidate who otherwise might turn out to be a solid hire.

to events to promote police careers? Are individuals in the LGBTQ communities working with the agency to make it a more attractive employer for their communities?

Oliver (2014, p. 43) describes six general benefits of engaging the community in the process of recruiting and selecting candidates:[18]

- More can be accomplished together that either group could accomplish alone.
- Working together will prevent duplication of individual or group efforts.
- Collaboration will enhance the power of advocacy and resource development.
- Joint efforts create more public visibility for the recruitment process.
- Community involvement will provide a more systematic and comprehensive approach to the recruitment and selection challenges.
- Working together on the initiative could create more opportunities for collaboration on future projects.

Hire People Who Can Police in an Unbiased Fashion

As discussed above, the first objective for agencies in the realm of recruitment and hiring is to produce a police force that represents the community. The second objective for agencies—to hire individuals who can police in an unbiased fashion—is not new, but the science of bias helps to inform our efforts. The science indicates that agencies will want to prioritize for hire those applicants who:

- Do not manifest explicit biases
- Have a history of positive interactions with diverse groups
- Are willing to reflect on and manage their own human biases.

Many agencies make some effort to identify people with explicit biases. Most common is to have the background investigators ask questions of people who know the applicant about the person's comments or actions that might reflect overt biases. The background investigation might involve a review of the applicant's social media to identify affiliations, contacts, or comments that might indicate bias issues. Some agencies include bias measures in their psychology testing, such as including the "Tolerance" sub-scale of the California Psychological Inventory or the "Prejudice" scale of the Minnesota Multiphasic Personality Inventory (MMPI).

Prioritizing individuals who have a history of positive interactions with diverse groups reflects the contact theory, described in Chap. 2. Recall that, per the contact theory, positive interaction with diverse groups can reduce both explicit and implicit biases. Like other selection criteria, this factor would be considered in conjunction with the multiple other factors to determine a person's suitability for hire. The San Francisco Police Department (SFPD) added two items to the initial written

---

[18]Referencing the COPS/IACP Leadership Project (2009).

form that individuals submit with their applications. One asked about the extent to which they were exposed to diverse individuals up to and through high school and the second asked the same for post high school. Similarly, the Kalamazoo P.D. assesses applicants' experience with diverse groups. This experience might come from an upbringing in a diverse area, paid or volunteer work in a diverse environment, military experience, and so forth. The applicants with this experience get some points added onto a passing written exam score. In Cheektowaga, in the interview, applicants are asked, "As a Police Officer you constantly have contact with people who have diverse cultures and backgrounds. Are there any situations where you have worked with people who have different backgrounds or cultures to achieve a common goal?"

The science suggests that agencies should hire people with the ability and motivation to reflect on and manage their biases. The Toronto Police Service "PACER Report" (Toronto Police Service 2013, Executive Summary p. 14) states, "All recruitment and hiring strategies must address bias by ensuring people hired by the Service are able to recognize their own biases and prevent them from influencing their professional responsibilities …" Screening on this basis, however, can present challenges. Applicants can be asked about biases in personal interviews, but a person with even minimal savvy, will be able to provide the socially desirable response to questions such as "what biases do you have?" The Kalamazoo P.D. (KPD) includes an interview question that requires a discussion about bias. This scenario that reflects "profiling by proxy"[19] comes from the FIP training program and reads:

> An elderly White lady in an all-White neighborhood calls the police to report a suspicious person out front in a car. It appears that the only thing that is suspicious is that the person in the car is a Black male. The woman does not articulate anything indicating criminal activity. Talk to me about this incident, the factors you would consider and what decision you might make.

According to KPD Chief Hadley, he is not looking for any one "right answer," but rather the thinking process of the person. For instance, can the applicant reflect on the woman's biases? Does s/he have empathy for the man in the car? What factors does s/he consider in making a decision? Chief Hadley reports that one lateral applicant referred to the Black man in the car as one of "those people" and said he would immediately suspect drug activity. He was not hired.

Another question option (in an interview or as part of a written submission) makes the assumption that everyone has biases: "Describe an incident/occurrence in which one of your biases manifested. How did it play out and would you act differently today if you got to do it over?" Again, the hiring entity would listen for the person's ability to acknowledge his/her own biases, and also his/her commitment to produce bias-free behavior.

---

[19]"Profiling by proxy" refers to the circumstance wherein community members' requests for police assistance reflect their own biases.

But relevant here, too, is the adage referenced above, "don't screen on what you can train." If an agency identifies a mature, well-intentioned individual who truly wants to serve the community, s/he can be trained, through a science-based curriculum, to recognize his/her biases and reduce and manage them.

Guard Against Implicit Biases in Managerial Decisions

There is considerable research documenting bias in employment-related decisions (for an overview, see Staats 2014; Staats et al. 2015; see also, Bertrand et al. 2005; Bertrand and Mullainathan 2004; Carlsson and Rooth 2007; Riach and Rich 2002; Wood et al. 2009).[20] These decisions might pertain to hiring, promotion, evaluation, raises, discipline, and other matters. As an example, one method researchers have used to assess hiring biases is to send cover letters and resumes to companies that are advertising for jobs (see e.g., Bendick et al. 1996; Bertrand and Mullainathan 2004). Pairs of letter/resumes are sent out that are identical, except for the gender or the race of the supposed applicant and then the researchers measure the response. Consistently, this research has found gender and race bias in the response to applicants (Carlsson and Rooth 2007; Bertrand et al. 2005; Bertrand and Mullainathan 2004; Riach and Rich 2002).

Fiske and Krieger (2013) reviewed some of the research showing how implicit biases can impact employment-related decisions and then summarized the "problems" and "solutions." Although these two authors focused on gender bias, their "problems" and "solutions" have application to other type of biases.

Problems

The first key problem these authors note is that even *well-intentioned managers* who are wholly committed to diversity and equal opportunity have implicit biases that can impact their decision-making. According to Fiske and Krieger (2013, p. 52):

> Employment decision makers ... cannot always act rationally, because, even if they consciously support equal opportunity norms, the subtle, unexamined forms of gender bias may prevent them from accurately perceiving decision-relevant information or optimally using it to make employment decisions. That is, managers might explicitly endorse equal opportunity, but unexamined prejudices might nevertheless derail their decisions.

The authors note that most individuals believe themselves to be less biased than the average person (Pronin et al. 2002; Pronin and Schmidt 2013) and, of course,

---

[20]The research cannot necessarily distinguish between explicit and implicit biases as the cause.

we cannot all be "above average."[21] Fiske and Krieger also suggest that the higher one is in an agency, the more at risk s/he is of manifesting bias; they explain (p. 57): "Power disinhibits behavior, making people monitor themselves less and operate on automatic more."

Fiske and Krieger reference a second problem, that I will call the "we-they" bias (this is more commonly referred to in the academic literature as outgroup bias). (Of course, one person's "we" and "they" is different from the next person's.) Research shows that we prefer and are more comfortable with people who we perceive are like ourselves (e.g., Brewer 1979; Hertel and Kerr 2001; Tajfel 1982) and, according to Fiske and Krieger (2013, p. 55), "When people categorize another person as one of 'us,' they automatically recognize positive traits more rapidly than when they categorized another person as one of 'them'" (citing the research of Perdue et al. 1990).

A third problem is that humans can give the same characteristic or behavior different attributions depending on the demographics of the individual being assessed and the biases associated with those demographics. They cite the following examples (Fiske and Krieger 2013, p. 54):

> … (W)hen behavior is tagged by gender, its interpretations shift: tagged as female, warm behavior is motherly; tagged as male, it is socially skilled. Aggressive behavior, tagged as male, might be assertive, but tagged as female might be bitchy.

A fourth problem related to managerial decisions is that we tend to interpret ambiguous information to confirm our own biases (e.g., Dovidio and Gaertner 2000; Hilton and Van Hippel 1996). This might, for instance, apply to an evaluation of an employee. For instance, the authors convey, when male employees do well at a "traditionally masculine task," this might be attributed by the evaluator to the man's inherent abilities. But when a female employee does well at the same sort of task, the evaluator may attribute that success to "chance or circumstance."[22]

A fifth problem is that we can, without awareness, shift our evaluation priorities in a manner consistent with our biases. As an example, a decision-maker may initiate the assessment of job applicants or people vying for promotion with a focus on *education*, but then shift his/her emphasis to *experience* when s/he comes across a female or racial/ethnic minority with strong education credentials.[23]

In summarizing the problems that place managers at risk, Fiske and Krieger (2013) remind us that bias isn't always "against" a group, it can be bias "for." And small, subtle, and periodic advantages can accrue to the "in group" over time. The authors explain that agency bias might take the form of "seemingly insignificant forms of preference or lenience towards members of one particular group" (p. 59). In a police department, these "seemingly insignificant" advantages (e.g., the plum

---

[21]Rachlinski et al. (2009) asked a group of judges to rank their own ability to "avoid racial prejudice in decision-making" relative to their peers. Ninety-seven percent placed themselves in the top half and 50 % placed themselves in the top quartile.

[22]Citing Deaux and Emswiller (1974), Swim and Sanna (1996).

[23]Citing Norton et al. (2004), Uhlmann and Cohen (2005).

assignment, the training opportunity) could produce significantly different career trajectories for the ingroup versus outgroup(s) over time.

Solutions

Fortunately, Fiske and Krieger (2013) follow their summary of problems with a list of potential solutions. These include:

- Prioritize diversity as an agency goal and monitor progress with data.
- Educate decision makers about how implicit bias can impact their judgements and destigmatize the discussion of bias in the workplace.
- Generate clear, objective criteria to be used for managerial decisions (hiring, promotion, evaluation), provide decision makers with information on the candidates that is linked to those criteria and require managers to explain their decisions based on those criteria.

Fiske and Krieger also suggest that, within employment settings, efforts should be undertaken to blur the lines that separate "in groups" from "outgroups." (This reflects the "blurring the lines" bias-reducing concept introduced in Chap. 2.) That is, instead of reinforcing group lines based on, for instance, gender, racial categories, and/or LGBT status, an organization should foster "group identities" that are more "pragmatic." Agencies might change a culture that defines the "in group" in terms of demographics (e.g., White males), to one that prioritizes, for instance, the highly productive patrol teams. This suggestion has interesting applications to police agencies; it raises the question of whether demographic associations within some agencies (e.g., Black Officers Association, Female Officers Association) have a downside by *reinforcing*, rather than *blurring*, lines. While this should be recognized, it could well be the case that those associations have sufficient benefits that offset this potential negative.

Another solution is based on the "we-they" bias mentioned above. That we all have such a bias, has implications for deciding who in an agency will make particular managerial decisions, such as reviewing job applicants or promotion files. If a single individual implements this process or the group making these decisions is made up individuals who share a common "we-they" identity (e.g., they are all White males with some college), the outcomes could be flawed. After sharing this "we-they" bias in a Fair and Impartial Policing command-level session for a small agency, the leadership decided that, instead of having a single individual—a White male sergeant— conduct the initial screening of job applicants, it would designate a group of diverse individuals to conduct the task. Presumably this "diverse group" would bring in a variety of "we-they" biases that could produce more egalitarian results.

This section on recruitment, hiring and promotions highlighted three important objectives that will help to produce fair and impartial agencies and agencies perceived to be same. An agency wants to recruit and hire individuals who represent the diversity of the community, hire people who can police in an unbiased fashion, and guard against implicit biases in hiring, promotion, evaluations, and other managerial decisions.

Training

Around the country, traditional racial-profiling training programs have reflected outdated understandings about prejudice; pursuant to the old paradigm, the emphasis has been on explicit biases. Hardin and Banaji (2013, p. 13) characterized the training that would be appropriate for reducing prejudice if dealing with *explicit* bias: "prejudice is best addressed by changing the hearts and minds of individuals." Consistent with their description, some training in the US for police has conveyed the message, "stop being prejudiced" with an emphasis on reducing animus toward stereotyped groups.[24] From the science, we now know that the old message is ill-suited for most individuals in modern society, including most individuals in policing, who do not have explicit biases. Further and more importantly, individuals receiving such old-school messages can be offended—producing a backlash against these efforts.[25]

Not only is the old school training offensive, it is inadequate in addressing biases as they manifest in modern society. According to Dovidio et al. (2000, p. 141):

> Approaches for dealing with the traditional form of prejudice are generally less effective for combating the consequences of contemporary forms. For example, Whites already consciously endorse egalitarian, nonprejudicial views and disavow traditional stereotypes. Moreover, the traditional approach of emphasizing social norms that proscribe the avoidance of negative behavior toward Blacks and other people of color is not likely to be effective for addressing (implicit bias). People possessing this type of bias have already internalized these norms and are very guarded about overtly discriminating against people of color.

The science calls for training that educates individuals on implicit bias and provides them with skills to be fair and impartial. And, as described in Chap. 2 of this book, the science indicates that motivated individuals *can be trained* to reduce

---

[24]Some of this training might come under the label "cultural sensitivity training," which comes in varied forms. Some are quite good and could complement and reinforce science-based bias training. As previewed in Chap. 2, high quality cultural sensitivity training could, for instance, provide stereotype-disconfirming information about "outgroups" and promote positive contact between police and members of those groups; recall, that both of these mechanisms can be bias-reducing.

[25]A "case study" of sorts comes from an individual who participated in February 2015 in a Fair and Impartial Policing Training-of-Trainers (TOT) session. He had recently been through a "traditional" racial profiling course that he characterized as the way this topic "should not be taught." He wrote on his FIP training evaluation that, because of his recent training experience, "(I) wanted nothing to do with FIP or its philosophy. As fate would have it I was 'hand-picked' to attend the train-the-officer classes and forced to go after presenting every excuse I could come up with to be excused. I came in Monday as opposed and defensive as I could covertly be without getting into trouble .... It took about two hours and I was sold on the theory of the class and wondering why I had not been through this training sooner."

and manage their biases. The Fair and Impartial Policing Training Program, produced with the support of USDOJ funds, has five training programs for police agencies. They are targeted toward: (1) academy recruits and/or in-service patrol officers, (2) first-line supervisors, (3) mid-managers (above first-line supervisor and below command-level), (4) command-level individuals, and (5) trainers.

The three-module curricula for academy recruits and in-service patrol officers helps participants:

- Understand that even well-intentioned people have biases that can impact their perceptions and behavior;
- Understand that policing based on stereotypes/biases is ineffective, unsafe, and unjust;
- Understand the consequences of biased policing for community members and the police agency; and,
- Acquire skills that help him/her reduce and manage biases.

Module 1 introduces the trainees to the science of bias and—through role plays, videos, and exercises—makes the point that *policing based on stereotypes is ineffective, unsafe and unjust.* Module 2 discusses the negative impact that biased policing has on individual community members and on the police agency. The latter discussion is linked to the concept of legitimacy—referring to the public view that police are "legitimate legal authorities, entitled to be obeyed" (Tyler 2004: 84). Community members who perceive the police as legitimate are more likely to comply with the law, cooperate with the police, and support the police (Sunshine and Tyler 2003; Tyler 1990, 2004; Tyler et al. 2015). The trainees are then instructed in skills they can use to produce trust, confidence, and legitimacy—with an emphasis on the core elements of procedural justice.

The skills imparted to the recruits and patrol officers in Module 3 to produce fair and impartial policing are:

- Recognize your implicit biases and implement "controlled" (that is, unbiased) behavior.
- Avoid "profiling by proxy"[26]
- Analyze your options with a fair and impartial policing lens
- Reduce ambiguity by slowing things down when feasible[27]
- Reduce ambiguity by engaging with the community.[28]

---

[26]As above, "profiling by proxy" references the situation wherein a community member calls the police because s/he has a bias. An example is implied by the scenario shared above: *an elderly White lady calls the police because there is "a suspicious person out front in a car." She conveys that the person is a black male and does not articulate any information that indicates criminal activity.*

[27]This reflects the previously shared scientific finding that lack of time (as well as cognitive busyness) can aggravate implicit biases and biased behavior.

[28]This skill harnesses the power of the contact theory.

The training for **first-line supervisors** (e.g., sergeants) starts with the science of bias and skills for reducing and managing biases, and then (a) addresses how to identify subordinates who may be acting in a biased manner—including those well-meaning officers whose biased behavior may not be consciously produced; (b) provides guidance to supervisors on how they should respond to officers who exhibit biased policing behaviors; (c) challenges trainees to think about how bias might manifest in their own behavior; and (d) provides guidance on how to speak about bias to individuals (e.g., officers, individual community members) and community groups. Key elements of this content are reflected in the section below on supervision.

In the command-level training, attendees are introduced to the science of bias and the Comprehensive Program to Produce Fair and Impartial Policing. Mid-Managers receive training that is a hybrid of the supervisor and command sessions. A train-the-trainer session teaches law enforcement instructors to implement both the recruit academy/patrol officers' and the first-line supervisors' training programs.

Because the traditional training on "racial profiling" has been based on outdated notions of how bias manifests, many seasoned law enforcement officers enter FIP training defensive, or even hostile. They expect the same messages and finger-pointing, but then start to relax once they hear the "modern" message based on current science. Reducing this defensiveness is key to promoting change within agencies.

Use-of-Force Training

In the second chapter of this book, on the science, three lines of research were presented that pertained to officers' split-second decisions to use force. The first line of research indicates the officers, like other people, have implicit biases linked to who is considered a threat (e.g., the Black-crime implicit bias); this human bias could produce a greater tendency to use force against individuals of color compared to Whites. A second line of studies indicate the potential of high-quality use-of-force training for reducing the impact of human biases on these split-second decisions. The third line of research indicates that officers could be impacted by a social/political atmosphere producing strong concerns about legal and other consequences of using force against racial/ethnic minorities. This "counter-bias" could lead police to put themselves in danger by slowing their response to an armed Black. As indicated above, all of these forces could be at work, depending on the individual officer, the agency training and the local and national "atmosphere."

There are interventions related to the findings of each line of research. Related to the first line of research, recognizing human biases in law enforcement, the profession—like any profession—needs to reduce implicit biases in their personnel. Mechanisms for reducing and managing biases were addressed in Chap. 2 of this book and, in this section on training, I described how training (such as the Fair and

Impartial Policing training program) could bring the science of implicit bias to pre-service and in-service personnel. Additionally, in the section on recruitment and hiring, I discussed how agencies might screen out individuals who have explicit biases and, instead, hire people who can police in an unbiased fashion.

To address "counter bias" (as referenced in the third line of research), police personnel need to believe that they will not face dire consequences when they legitimately defend themselves or others against the threat of serious bodily injury or death. They need to have the confidence that they will be supported by their leadership and by community members in their use of reasonable force. This is no small task in this post-Ferguson era wherein trust in police is at its lowest level in 22 years (Jones 2015), each incident involving police use of deadly force (particularly if the subject is a racial/ethnic minority) is perceived by many community stakeholders to be unreasonable until proven otherwise, and the prosecution of police for on-duty, fatal, shootings is up 366 % (Dewan and Williams 2015). Producing this confidence on the part of officers will require considerable (and likely long-term) efforts as the police and community work to heal the breech between them. Guidance comes from various resources including the President's Task Force on Twenty-First Century Policing and documents produced by the major police organizations such as IACP (see e.g., IACP 2015), and guidance comes from other sections of this chapter (e.g., community outreach, operations).

But interestingly and importantly, the implications for *police use-of-force training* are the same for all three lines of research. As previewed in Chap. 2, agencies must ensure that their personnel have frequent exposure to scenario-judgement training wherein counterstereotypes are portrayed in ambiguous-threat situations in various environments. The key outcome of this training is to condition officers such that demographics do not inappropriately impact their force decisions.

Several concepts from the science of bias described in Chap. 2 provide guidance on how this training can reduce or eliminate bias when making force decisions. The first two relevant concepts are counterstereotypes and ambiguity. Recall that, with regard to the first concept, in the training scenarios, the person who turns out to be a threat to the officer should just as likely be a woman as a man, a Caucasian as a person of color, an older person as a younger person, a well-dressed person as one who is not, and so forth. (And it is equally as important that the person who turns out to be a *non-threat* also represents a counterstereotype.) With this exposure over time, the law enforcement officer learns that demographics are "non-diagnostic" for threat (that is, it weakens the stereotype activation) and the officer then focuses on other clues, such as hands and behavior.[29, 30]

---

[29]The science-based elements of scenario-based training can be applied to nonvideo training, too, such as Simunitions, wherein the "opponent" demographics are absent due to the mask. Implicit bias theory would not support this training in terms of its ability to reduce biases, but arguably such training could lead officers to focus on clues to threat other than demographics.

[30]Correll et al. (2014) also highlighted the importance of high-intensity training because "low-intensity training may not be sufficient to eliminate bias outside the lab." Video training "intensity" might be increased with the "shoot back" capabilities of some systems.

To be most effective, the scenarios should place these counterstereotypes in *ambiguous-threat* situations. Recall, the distinction made in Chap. 2, when I discussed the disproportionate friendly fire against officers of color. If the threat is unambiguous—for instance, the officer is facing a pointed gun—it is unlikely that demographics (and associated stereotypes) will impact his/her decision. It is when the threat is *ambiguous* that the risk of implicit biases is greatest. An example is the shooting by the officer in Columbia, South Carolina in 2014. The state trooper pulled over a young Black male and, after the man was out of the car, asked him for his driver's license. The young man quickly turned and reached into the car. The officer, clearly fearful, fired. This ambiguous behavior on the part of a Black male produced perceptions of threat; likely if a professionally dressed, White woman had acted the same way, the perception (and outcome) would have been different.[31]

Another science-of-bias concept introduced earlier has application to producing use-of-force scenarios for judgment training. Recall that Correll et al. (2011) found that *context*—in terms of neighborhood crime—impacted the activation of biases. The implication of their research is that, for maximum effect on implicit biases, the scenarios that officers experience should place stereotype threats and counterstereotype threats in backdrops that vary in terms of the crime-environment.

Police readers will recognize that scenarios described above exist in the sets provided by commercial providers (or produced by the agencies themselves); some scenarios for judgement training reflect counterstereotypes in ambiguous-threat situations in various crime environments. The questions are these: What proportion of officers are exposed to this method of training? And, for those who *are* exposed to it—is their exposure to it frequent enough to produce the desired conditioning effects? Not all agencies have access to video-scenario training and, of those that do, many only have the resources (including the resources required to take officers off the street for training) to provide minimal exposure to scenarios each year.[32]

Research by Morrison and Garner (2011) indicates that fewer than half of agencies provide computer-based scenario training and, of those that *do* provide the training, one-quarter expose their personnel to only one scenario annually. (Six in 10 expose their officers to fewer than 4 scenarios annually.) And we cannot assume that the few scenarios to which officers are exposed contain the elements described above. Again, we do not know empirically "how much is enough" and that research is needed, but, in the meantime, we can recall the common-sense conjecture of Blair

---

[31] A dash-cam video of this shooting was found on 12/14/2015 at http://www.wltx.com/story/news/local/2014/09/24/video-released-released-of-trooper-involved-shooting/16187305/.

[32] In Sanford (FL), when the video-scenario equipment was broken, the use-of-force trainer would send an in-service officer into a room armed with a fake gun whereupon s/he encountered four people of various races and genders. Each of the four individuals reached for an item at the same time; one of them reached for a gun. The officer had to identify and respond appropriately to the threat. Like the scenarios described above, officers, who went through this exercise several times, could only succeed if they ignored demographics. In a variation of this training, the officer engages in rigorous physical exercise before entering the room, to increase stress.

et al. (2001) reported in Chap. 2: the more exposures one gets over time (e.g., to judgment scenarios), the more likely it is to produce "long-lasting changes" (p. 838).

Supervision

The men and women who comprise the agency's top leadership can have great ideas and great wisdom and adopt strong policies, but their impact will be greatly reduced if the first-line supervisors are not on board with regard to their implementation and application. As shared with me by David Romine, former chief of St. Pete Beach Police Department, "policy succeeds or fails at the first line supervisor" (personal communication, 15 March 2010). This statement is true for efforts to promote fair and impartial policing. We must ask the first-line supervisors to "supervise to promote fair and impartial policing" and we must provide them with the information and skills they need to do this. As previewed above, we need to train first-line supervisors so that they understand:

- How bias manifests in even well-intentioned people
- How to identify officers who may be manifesting bias
- How to respond when they believe that biased policing might be occurring
- How bias might manifest in their own work and decisions
- How to talk about bias with individuals and groups.

The first bullet reflects education in the modern science of bias. Then first-line supervisors need to think about how bias might manifest in their subordinates—in the ill-intentioned (e.g., racist) officers, but also in those who have the best of intentions but, like the rest of us, have human biases. Trying to identify the ill-intentioned officers with explicit biases is not new. While police departments vary considerably with regard to the intensity of their efforts to seek out such individuals, often the cues are there to be unearthed. That a person has explicit biases—against racial minorities, low-income individuals, Muslims, the undocumented, or other groups—might be conveyed verbally (in the break room, on the radio, off duty, in the jokes s/he tells) or in his/her behavior on the job. Regarding the latter, law enforcement officers report that they know who the racists are (and others with explicit biases); if it is not a secret to their colleagues, it should not be unknown to the attentive supervisor. It should be made clear to this person manifesting explicit biases that biased speech and behavior is unacceptable, and continued noncompliance should result in appropriate discipline up to and including termination.

Bias will also manifest in well-intentioned individuals and supervisors must be attentive to this, as well. In the FIP training for first-line supervisors, the attendees can easily report what a strong Black-crime implicit bias might look like in one of their subordinates. He might engage with African-American males as if they are all criminals; he might request consent to search from them although in the same circumstances, but with another demographic group, the officer would not; he might be more likely ask "where are you coming from" or "are you on probation or parole"; he might be more verbally or physically aggressive. Supervisors in training classes easily identify possible behaviors of a subordinate who thinks wealthy individuals are law abiding and honest. She might not frisk the wealthier individual even when indications of a threat are present. If there is a two-car crash where the two drivers have different stories—blaming each other, this officer might be inclined to believe the man with the tie and the BMW, not the man in overalls driving a beat-up truck.

Supervisors have various sources of information that they use when monitoring their subordinates for good and bad behavior. These same sources of information can be useful when "scanning" to see if officers might be practicing biased policing; further, these might be the supplemental sources to which a supervisor turns once s/he has an initial suspicion that biased behavior might be occurring. A supervisor's concern that an individual might be manifesting implicit bias might come from observing the officer in the field or on video, reading his reports, listening to radio transmissions, viewing MDT transmissions, reviewing external/internal complaints and so forth. The supervisor might get information from other officers. Once a supervisor has an initial concern, maybe based on a single source, s/he might turn to the other sources of information to see if there is information that affirms or negates the concern.

Although the supervisor has various sources of information to help him/her scan for and identify biased behavior, it is important to recognize the challenge associated with proving (or *disproving*, for that matter) biased policing. Behavior is biased if the officer's *motivation* involves the inappropriate consideration of race or other demographics. Two officers might exhibit the same behavior and one officer's behavior may be biased and the other's not. This highlights the challenge for supervisors who are "supervising to promote fair and impartial policing." We must recognize that this supervisor will rarely have definitive information indicating bias. More often s/he will be dealing with ambiguous information—information that may *indicate* biased policing, but is not proof of it.[33]

This challenge (of ambiguous information) does not give supervisors license to abandon this important task, but it does have implications for what supervisors can and should do if they suspect biased behavior. With evidence that would not reach the required level of proof to sustain a complaint, the supervisor must intervene in an informal manner. The supervisor might present to the officer the information that she has pulled together from several sources. She would ask the subordinate what he makes of it; and, in fact, there *may be a bias-free explanation* for what the supervisor has observed. If there is not a bias-free explanation, the supervisor would convey her concern—highlighting how the potentially biased behavior, even if unintentional, could impact negatively the officer's goals to be effective, safe, and

---

[33]In the section on agency policy, I highlighted the importance of "enforcement language" that will allow, even encourage, supervisors to intervene informally when the information is ambiguous.

just. The tone of this conversation must be nonaccusatory and the likelihood of success will be increased if the officer has been exposed to the new paradigm. An officer still working under the auspices of the old paradigm will perceive he is being called a racist (if a race allegation) and could easily become defensive; an officer exposed to the new paradigm will be more likely to recognize this intervention as one focusing on biases that we all have. And even if the conversation does not produce the light bulb response ("thanks, Sarge!") to which the supervisor aspires, it may plant a seed and prompt the officer to think about how he needs to be more fair and impartial.

The more supervisors talk informally about human biases and biased policing, the easier such discussions become. Supervisors at roll call trainings might remind officers of the new paradigm to which they were introduced in training by posing questions such as those described above. "What would a Black-crime implicit bias look like in an officer, even a well-meaning one?" "What would a bias against homeless or transgender individuals look like?" In fact, the supervisor could develop a hypothetical that actually reflects what he suspects is biased behavior on the part of a particular subordinate—without naming her, of course. This individual might recognize herself in the example and make changes on her own.

Supervisors must also reflect on how their own biases might manifest in their work. Their biases could impact their operational decisions or on their managerial decisions. Examples of operational decisions that could be impacted by bias include making decisions about what part of the unit's geographical area should get more or less coverage, in what areas aggressive tactics are allowed, and what crimes to enforce vigorously what crimes to ignore. Examples of managerial decisions that could be impacted by biases include whom to assign to the high activity areas, whom to recommend for promotion or special training, and whom to give the plum assignments. In FIP training sessions, female supervisors have no problem describing what it might look like if a supervisor thought that female officers were less capable than men: "The supervisor will not assign two females to work together." "The supervisor will not place the female in the high-crime areas." "The supervisor will not recommend the female for promotion, despite evidence indicating her equivalent or superior performance." "He will not designate a female when he needs a unit leader in his absence."

Supervisors need to be able to speak to individual community members and groups about bias and allegations of bias. A common situation involving an individual community member is when a subordinate is accused of biased policing and the supervisor is called to the scene. First of all, our suggested response from that accused officer would recognize the allegation made by the person, but then get right back to the business of the stop. The recognition could be in the form of "I understand that you feel that way" or "I'm sorry that you feel that way." Getting back to business would sound like, "I pulled you over because you were going 50 mph in a 35 mph zone." Having an argument on the side of the road as to whether the police action was biased is not productive.

But what if the tension is not reduced and the supervisor is now called to the scene? As many good supervisors know, just listening to a community member can go a long way toward reducing tension, and sometimes the incident ends with the community member satisfied just because s/he was heard. If the community member continues in his/her agitation and accusation, then the supervisor directs that person to the formal complaint process. The supervisor should not adjudicate on the scene; he should neither proclaim his officer's innocence (since the supervisor very likely does not know whether the behavior was biased or not) nor undermine him.

Accountability Measures to Promote Bias-Free Policing

All agencies have various accountability mechanisms to ensure that employees do what they are supposed to. Mechanisms like personnel evaluations, in-car or body-worn cameras, early-intervention systems, and the complaint system are used to make sure officers act within policy, ethically, and professionally. Agencies need to use these accountability mechanisms to promote fair and impartial policing as well.

One example of applying an accountability system to the bias-free-policing objective is the review of video from body-worn or in-car cameras. Virtually, all agencies with cameras have supervisors (or other personnel) view video from incidents that involve use of force, an injury, or a complaint, or produce an otherwise serious outcome. Some agencies are enhancing the "accountability strength" of these cameras by having supervisors review "random" video. For instance, a supervisor might be expected to review 45 min of "random" video for each direct report each month. That supervisor is scanning to ensure that the subordinate's behavior is in policy, professional, and ethical; the point here is that the supervisor should also be attending to fair and impartial policing. This "observation" information can be used with other sources of information to either assure the supervisor that his direct report is practicing fair and impartial policing, or may raise concerns or provide support for concerns that were precipitated by other evidence.

Employee evaluations represent another example of an opportunity for an agency to direct an existing accountability mechanism toward fair and impartial policing. The agency's evaluation might include reference to "Policing in a fair and impartial manner" or, more indirectly, "policing in a manner that promotes the public trust and confidence." This requires supervisors to attend to such behaviors and conveys to employees that these are valued aspects of their work.

While the complaint review system is a critically important accountability mechanism for police departments, special issues are raised when it comes to complaints of biased policing. The key issue was referenced above: *It is very difficult to prove (or disprove, for that matter) biased policing.* To understand this point, compare biased policing allegations to complaints of excessive force. An investigator in an internal or external complaint review entity who is investigating excessive force, can focus on *behavior*. What resistance did the subject manifest? What level of force was used in response? And where do the twain meet on the agency's use-of-force continuum? In contrast, the key transgression in biased policing is the *motivation* for the behavior. Two identical actions on the part of two officers might be biased policing in one, but not in the other.

During the period when the LAPD was implementing the provisions of their consent decree with the USDOJ, the LAPD Police Commission expressed great concern when, several years in a row, the department reported a significant number of biased policing complaints, but none that were sustained.[34] The Director of LAPD's Internal Affairs (IA) unit, Commander Rick Webb, sought to compare this experience to other departments nationwide. He and I called complaint review entities around the nation to find out their experience in receiving and sustaining biased policing complaints. We contacted both (a) systems internal to agencies, such as an Internal Affairs Unit; and (b) external systems, such as an independent civilian complaint review board. The modal experience was *zero complaints sustained*. We also asked the investigators whether the biased policing complaints were similar to or different from other categories of complaints. A sworn officer in an internal unit reported, "Profiling is intent based. Unless the officer confesses, it is almost impossible to prove. Often the complainant cannot point to any specific evidence of racial bias." Individuals working in external review organizations made these comments:

- "Bias is more subtle. That doesn't mean it is not there, but it's near impossible to determine when race is an inappropriate motivator in an incident."
- "The challenge is getting into the officer's head. The officer can come up with a reason other than race. Maybe he's lying, maybe he's not. Maybe the citizen is right, maybe s/he's not. For them (the citizen), it's just a feeling—likely based on past experiences. Sometimes they are just wrong and even if they are right, there is no objective proof."

Because of these constraints, community stakeholders should not evaluate an agency's commitment to fair and impartial policing based on sustained complaints. And more importantly, complaint review cannot be the centerpiece of an agency's efforts to promote bias-free policing. I have had chiefs tell me *just that* when asked what they are doing to address the national issue of biased policing. Response: "We take each and every complaint very seriously." I then ask how many complaints the agency has sustained, and the inevitable response is "zero."

Some agencies have adopted mediation for biased policing complaints. This option was raised in a command-level session I was holding in 2008 in Las Vegas for sworn and nonsworn individuals from agencies around the U.S. When we got to

---

[34]This concern was expressed again by the LA Police Commission in December of 2015 (Mather 2015).

the discussion of complaints, a deputy chief said, "indicative of how seriously we take these allegations, we process every one of them formally through Internal Affairs (IA)" (versus, for instance, processing them more informally through chain-of-command). Rich Rosenthal, who at the time was the civilian auditor for the Denver Police Department (DPD), reported that "the DPD takes the complaints so seriously that we try to process as many as we can through mediation." He explained that when they processed the complaints formally through IA, they got "zero sustained complaints, zero complainant satisfaction, and zero officer accountability." Their aspirations were not high; they sought a mechanism that could beat "zero," "zero," and "zero"—and adopted a mediation option for biased policing complaints.

With a mediation option, the agency develops a process whereby, if both parties agree, they can meet with an independent, trained mediator to discuss the allegations/incident. The agency will need to develop a policy about who can participate and under what circumstances and will need to provide incentives for officers to participate (otherwise, "zero, zero, zero" might be *just fine* for many). LAPD adopted a mediation option for complaints, including biased policing complaints in 2014. The program is described as an "informal, confidential process in which the complainant(s) and accused employee(s) meet face-to-face and, with the assistance of a neutral mediator, discuss the alleged misconduct with the goal of arriving at a mutually agreeable resolution." That "mutually agreeable resolution" might be to "agree to disagree." The process is voluntary and confidential, and once convened it is the only avenue for resolution.[35] Although the program is still rather new at the time of this writing, it has attracted a number of pairs of complainants and officers, producing positive results. The LAPD process is too new to evaluate, but the Denver program has undergone evaluation. Proctor et al. (2009) reported that the Denver mediation option, compared to the traditional processing of complaints, was faster and produced greater community member and officer satisfaction. They also claimed that the mediation option had a more positive impact on future officer behavior (as measured by citizen complaints).

As above, the desired outcome is a "mutually agreeable resolution" even if it is an agreement to disagree. These encounters may not produce a meeting of the minds with regard to the bias complaint, but the process could still provide a constructive forum for sharing two perspectives and even for mutual education. Importantly, each gets to voice his/her perspective—which could be important to both the officer and the complainant. And then the complainant might learn that traffic stops by lone cops at night are always an "unknown" that leads to vigilant behavior—behavior that the complainant might have attributed to his own race. The officer, in turn, might learn about police behaviors that give rise to perceptions of bias.

---

[35]For some LAPD officers, the mediation option is preferable to the full IA review that could be a long and sometimes expensive process. For the IA process, many officers retain representation and are subject to questioning, not just about the bias complaint, but all other potential constitutional issues.

Measurement

Measurement of biased policing can be a part of an agency's efforts to promote fair and impartial policing. That said, police and community leaders need to be realistic about what measurement can and cannot tell us. This section is about the pros and cons, costs and benefits of attempts to measure biased policing—whether at the agency or individual officer level. Obviously, the ability to measure biased policing would be a great advancement to efforts to control it. Thinking of measurement at the *agency* level, the ideal scenario might be as follows: (1) an agency measures the existence of biased policing, (2) it implements interventions to promote fair and impartial policing, and (3) the agency again measures biased policing to assess the impact of efforts. At the *individual* level, the ideal is to measure biased policing on the part of each police professional and then intervene with the specific individuals who are shown to engage in biased practices; a follow-up measure of biased policing could affirm or not the effectiveness of the intervention.

Unfortunately, these aspirations do not match up with reality. In fact, it is very difficult to measure biased policing on the part of an agency or on the part of an individual police professional. This section will review some of the ways that researchers have tried to measure bias in policing and review the potential of those efforts, as well as the caveats.

The History and Role of Measurement

Modern attempts to measure biased policing take us back to the late 1990s and early 2000s when the issue of biased policing came back to the fore with the label "racial profiling." During that period, data collection became the "default" response of concerned agency executives and community stakeholders. It seemed to many individuals, at the time, to be the only tool in the toolbox; and, in fact, much of the discussion of agency efforts back then were focused on measurement; we were not giving attention to training, outreach, leadership, supervision and so forth. During that period, a number of agencies—willingly or under pressure—began to collect vehicle stop data in their quest to measure biased policing. Through these systems, officers submitted information (orally to dispatch, through the MDT, or on paper forms) on their vehicle stops—such as the perceived race, gender, and age of the subject; the location; the reason for the stop; whether or not a search was conducted; the result of the search; and the outcome of the stop.

During those early days, the sense was that this information would answer this question: Which agencies have a biased policing problem and which ones do not? While there can still be a role for data collection, we now know that these systems should not be used to answer that question as this assessment is contrary to the implications of the science of bias. *Every agency* (if it hires humans to do the job) has a biased policing issue and must, therefore, be proactive in producing fair and impartial policing. No agency can declare itself—with or without data—bias free.

So where does measurement fit today into an agency's efforts to promote fair and impartial policing? Agency leaders who decide to implement a Comprehensive Program to Produce Fair and Impartial Policing should consider the costs and benefits of measurement and make an informed decision (ideally, in concert with community leaders) regarding whether a measurement system will add value to the overall efforts. On the positive side, measurement systems can convey to the community a commitment to unbiased policing and, relatedly, a commitment to accountability and transparency. Such systems can provide the agency with information about what its personnel are doing (regardless of the race data)—answering such questions as: *How many stops do we make and where? How many searches do we conduct and with what result?* Data collection may deter biased policing as officers consider whom they are stopping and why.

But there are also negatives or "costs" associated with data collection. While it does not take much time for an officer to fill out a form for a vehicle stop, a worthy measurement effort will have quality control at the higher levels to avoid "garbage in, garbage out." Supervisors should be reviewing submissions to ensure that every targeted stop produces a form and that the data entries appear valid. There may be costs associated with data input, and agency personnel or outside contractors will be needed to analyze the data. Other potential negatives are irresponsible reporting of the results by the press and others, and de-policing on the part of officers.

A key aspect of the cost-benefit debate centers on this question: *What can we actually measure?* Such systems can absolutely measure "disparity." That is, for instance, a system can show whether people of color are stopped disproportionate to their representation in some comparison population—the "benchmark" population. What is much more challenging, is determining the *causes* or *sources* of that disparity. Some of that disparity may be produced by biased policing; some of that disparity may reflect other, legitimate, factors.

For instance, in the case of measuring vehicle stops, results indicating that one group is stopped disproportionately (a finding of "disparity"), could reflect biased policing, or that disparity might alternatively or additionally reflect legitimate factors such as variations across groups in the location, quality and quantity of driving. In the case of stop and frisks, results indicating that one group is stopped disproportionately, could reflect biased policing, or that disparity might alternatively or additionally reflect legitimate factors such as differential criminal behavior on the part of demographic groups, differential locations of demographic groups vis a vis police deployment, and so forth. The key point here is that "disparity" results (and I'm using that only in the social science sense) is not the same as bias. "Disparity" can be made up of bias, but also of nonbias factors, such as those listed above. For social scientists and others, it is easy to measure disparity; it is difficult, however, to parse out the factors that contribute to that disparity. This point has gotten lost in many discussions of biased policing measurement.

Vehicle Stop Data Collection: Assessing Who Is Stopped

As above, a popular form of measurement has been vehicle stop data collection. These systems have the pros and cons listed above. When it comes to the analysis of the data that have been collected, there are a variety of "benchmarks" that have been used to make sense of the data on who is stopped by police (see Fridell 2004, 2005). For instance, the agency's stop data may show that 70 % of its traffic stops are of Caucasians and 30 % are of people of color. Conceptually, the ideal benchmark would provide a similar breakdown by race that reflects "the people at risk of being stopped by police, assuming no bias." With such an ideal benchmark, we could see if, for instance, people of color are overrepresented among police stops relative to their representation among people who are at legitimate risk of being stopped, assuming no bias. Benchmarks that come closest to measuring those people "at risk," are in effect, "controlling" for the legitimate factors that might produce disparity. There are a variety of benchmarks that have been used by agencies and their social scientist partners and they vary considerably in terms of their quality. The weakest benchmark is residential population as measured by the U.S. Census; higher quality benchmarks include "Internal Benchmarking" and observation. Internal Benchmarking is described below. With the observation method, trained observers identify who is traveling through and/or violating traffic laws at a particular location to produce a benchmark for the stops at the same location. All of these benchmarks can measure disparity; the higher quality benchmarks are, by definition, better at ruling out the legitimate factors that might produce disparity, although none of them meets the ideal. Again, it is important to remember that *disparity is not necessarily bias.*

A book, *By the Numbers: A Guide for Analyzing Race Data from Vehicle Stops* (Fridell 2004), provides information on various benchmarks that have been used to try to make sense of vehicle stop data.[36] Most of these methods produce an assessment of disparity at the *agency* level (e.g., Census benchmarking, observation). One of the benchmarks, Internal Benchmarking, can be used to identify racial disparities in activities at the level of the *officer*. With this method, researchers compare officers' activities (e.g., vehicle stops, searches) to the activities of their similarly situated peers (that is, for instance, comparing the officer to other individuals working in the same area, with the same task assignment, on the same shift). Unfortunately, this method can only be used by large agencies because comparing officers to their similarly situated peers requires a sufficient sample size in those groups to draw conclusions. The advantage, however, is that it can be used to identify officers who are "outliers" in terms of the extent to which they intervene

---

[36]This book, the writing and publication of which was supported by the USDOJ Office of Community Oriented Policing Services, is available for free downloading from the PERF website at www.policeforum.org under "Publications" and "Free OnLine Documents." A summary version, on the same website, is Fridell (2005): "Understanding Race Data from Vehicle Stops: A Stakeholder's Guide."

(compared to their similarly situated peers) with, for instance, racial/ethnic minorities. Importantly, once an agency uses this method to identify "outliers," the investigation is only half-way done. There may very well be bias-free reasons for the disproportionate intervention and so the second step of an inquiry would explore those possibilities.

Geographic Units of Analysis to Assess Police Bias

Different "units of analysis" can be considered within measurement systems. Social scientists use the phrase "units of analysis" to refer to the entity being studied; for instance, a researcher might be studying individuals (e.g., the individual employees working at an agency), groups of individuals (e.g., patrol units), events (e.g., traffic stops), geographic areas (e.g., neighborhoods, states, countries), or maybe agencies (e.g., law enforcement agencies). To provide two examples, most vehicle stop studies have used "stops" (as a form of "event") as the unit of analysis. The data are collected about that stop, including the demographics of the individual who was stopped, time, location, reason for the stop, post-stop activities such as searches. In contrast, in the "internal benchmarking" method described above, the unit of analysis is individual officers.

In contrast to these units, some researchers analyzing data from vehicle stops or pedestrian police–civilian street encounters (such as NYPD stop and frisks), have used *geographic areas* as the unit of analysis.[37] These units have some advantages over other units; the key advantage is that, in examining police activities (that are in response to criminal behavior) within areas, the researcher can control for behavior (e.g., criminal behavior).

Why is this important? A decision by an officer to engage in, for instance, a detention (or "stop") and then, maybe, to conduct a frisk, is linked to suspicions of criminal behavior.[38] If a researcher were assessing bias in stop-and-frisk activities at the event (stop-and-frisk) level of analysis, s/he would be hindered by the inability to gather information on the behavior of the individuals that preceded (and supposedly justified) the stop. We would only have either the word of the officer or the word of the detained individual regarding whether the subject was engaging in suspicious activity that might warrant a detention. Neither of these sources would be sufficiently credible to most researchers (Gelman et al. 2007). Further, we would not know who in the area engaged in similar, suspicious behavior and was *not detained.*

---

[37]Methods for analyzing vehicle stops that use geographic units include Observation Benchmarking and Blind Enforcement Mechanisms. Both of these methods are discussed in *By the Numbers*.

[38]The "stop"/detention must be based on reasonable suspicion that criminal activity is afoot. Not all stops include a frisk. The frisk must be separately justified by the officer's reasonable belief that the person is armed and thus a potential danger to him/her.

Using the geographic area as the unit of analysis, however, allows the researcher to measure criminal behavior—not the criminal behavior of the individual, but the level of criminal behavior in the *area*. Thus, a researcher could assess the level of stop-and-frisks across areas, controlling for the level of crime; and if, for instance, one neighborhood populated by individuals of color had more stop-and-frisks than neighborhoods populated by Caucasians, even after crime was controlled, this would be a red flag for racially biased policing.[39]

To assess racial disparities in stop-and-frisks in New York City, Gelman et al. (2007) gathered for the 75 New York Police Department (NYPD) precincts both the stop-and-frisk rates and crime rates for the various racial/ethnic groups. They conducted their analyses for four categories of crimes: violent crimes, weapon offenses, property crimes, and drug crimes. They found that, for violent crimes and weapons offenses, Blacks and Hispanics were stopped almost twice as often as Whites even after race-specific crime rates were controlled.

While these results, indeed no results, will provide *conclusive proof* of police racial bias (indeed, the authors were cautious in their interpretation of *why* these disparities exist), these results do raise a serious red flag for potential biased policing and the methods reflect a high-quality example of the power of using geographic areas as a unit of analysis when attempting to assess bias in policing.

Searches

Within a vehicle or pedestrian stop measurement system, an agency might assess disparity with regard to actions on the part of officers that occur *after* the stop is made. Data can be analyzed with regard to whether a search was conducted and the result of that search (i.e., whether seizable evidence was found), the outcome of the stop (e.g., ticket, warning), the length of the stop, and so forth. A post-stop action that has gotten much attention in the measurement arena is searches. These analyses, too, are constrained by the capabilities of social science. The most common error on the part of agencies, activist groups and the press involves drawing conclusions about bias from search data. There are two ways to analyze search data: (1) "percent searched data," and (2) search hit rates. If "percent searched" is calculated, it would convey something like: 13 % of the Caucasians who were stopped by the police were searched and 20 % of the people of color who were stopped by the police were searched. In many reports and frequently in press coverage, these percentages are used erroneously to draw conclusions regarding racial bias. These data can be used to indicate *disparity* but, as above, disparity is not necessarily produced by bias. Drawing conclusions regarding the existence (or absence) of bias using percent searched data, is based on a faulty assumption that all people stopped by the police (in vehicles or on foot) are at equal, legitimate risk of being searched.

---

[39]See e.g., American Civil Liberties Union of Massachusetts (2014).

This is not the case and, indeed, even the US Supreme Court says otherwise.[40] Police bias might be one explanation for racial/ethnic disparities in percent-searched data, but an additional or alternative explanation for all or part of the disparity is that racial/ethnic groups are not represented proportionate to their representation in the population among the people at legitimate risk of being searched by police absent bias. It is understandable that certain segments of the population would be more likely to give police legitimate cause for a search. An analysis of "percent searched" for *any* agency's data would show, for instance, that men are searched more than women and young people are searched more than older people. These findings produce no outcry of biased policing, because people understand that men and young people are disproportionately involved in crime and therefore it is likely that they would be more likely to give police cause for a search. As discussed in Chap. 2, criminological research shows that people of color are disproportionately represented among people who commit street crimes relative to their representation among the population. As such, we should not be surprised that they are disproportionately represented among the people who are searched by police.

In contrast to the "percent searched" analysis described above, the search "hit rates" can, in some analyses, provide more worthy information regarding police bias. In calculating "hit rates," we learn what percentage of the searches of various groups produced seizable evidence. Thus, for instance, an analysis might show that 20 % of the searches of Caucasians produced seizable evidence, compared to 13 % of the searches of racial and ethnic minorities. While not conclusive, such findings are a red flag for bias, because the search hit rate for racial/ethnic minorities is *lower* than that of Caucasians (Ayres 2002). A full explanation of why this is a red flag (based on the "outcome test" in economic theory), why it is not conclusive, and the appropriate analyses to produce meaningful findings[41] is contained in the publication mentioned above: *By the Numbers: A Guide for Analyzing Race Data from Vehicle Stops* (Fridell 2004).[42]

Making Decisions About Measurement

Measurement is not just about social science; it is about accountability, community relations, and politics, as well. An executive who seems unwilling to recognize the reality of bias in policing may be more likely to face calls from community

---

[40]See for instance, Terry versus Ohio, 302 U.S. 1 (1968).

[41]Importantly, these analyses, based on the outcome theory in economics, can be conducted on only a subset of police searches. See Fridell (2004).

[42]Gelman et al. (2007) calculate another form of "hit rate" in their analysis of "stop-and-frisk" data in New York City. They assess the proportion of detentions that result in an arrest to measure the "efficiency" of stops. In finding a lower arrest hit rate for minorities, they suggest that the stops of Whites are more efficient and, conversely, the stops of racial/ethnic minorities is more indiscriminate (p. 820).

members to adopt a measurement system, and maybe he *should* face these demands. The hope on the part of the community members is that the disparity findings will put pressure on the executive to take the issue seriously. On the other hand, the executive who publicly recognizes the reality of bias in policing and is willing to take steps to promote fair and impartial policing, might not get that call and maybe he shouldn't be so pressured. As above, such an executive (along with his community partners) might decide that data collection does not provide bang-for-the-buck value alongside the other efforts. Data collection imperfectly *measures* biased policing; all the other components of the Comprehensive Program described here actually *do something about it*. It is legitimate therefore, in an era of finite resources, to decide that resources might more effectively be dedicated to, for instance, training, instead of measurement.

Related to this calculation, is a conversation I had with a state legislator. The members of this state's Racial Profiling Task Force were educated on the modern science of bias and the Comprehensive Program to Produce Fair and Impartial Policing. Many on the task force wanted to devote resources to elements *other than measurement*, but one state legislator was adamant that agencies in the state collect vehicle stop data. I asked her this, "If we implemented data collection and found racial/ethnic stop disparities in the city of X, what would you want to happen?" She replied, "I'd want the Chief of X to implement a Comprehensive Program to Produce Fair and Impartial Policing." I replied: "But the Chief of X is already committed to implementing a comprehensive response." So the legitimate question: What is the value added of measurement in such a situation?

But even imperfect measurement can enhance accountability and community trust. LaVigne et al. (2014, p. 28) describe the officer-level accountability associated with documentation of stop and frisks:

> ...Requiring officers to document each stop (including the reason for and outcome of the stop) acts as an accountability measure in and of itself because it compels officers to justify their activity immediately after it has taken place. By requiring officers to fill out a form detailing their activities, this measure also makes it more costly for officers to conduct stops, which will incentivize them to do so only when they believe it is necessary and appropriate.

At the agency level, data on, for instance, stops and frisks can provide important information, even if it produces an imperfect measure of bias in policing. As LaVigne et al. (2014) argue, these data can aid the agency in determining whether there are certain activities that have a disparate *impact* on subsets of their population (e.g., as defined by race, income, geographic location). While this disparate impact is not proof of inappropriate policing, it might lead to further inquiry and maybe even problem-solving to address the underlying issues that produce the disparate outcomes.[43]

---

[43]An excellent report examining racial disparities in bicycle stops and citations on the part of the Tampa (FL) P.D. is Ridgeway et al. 2016.

Every jurisdiction implementing a Comprehensive Program to Produce Fair and Impartial Policing should evaluate whether measurement would be a valuable add-on to those efforts. An agency's leader and his/her concerned community members should assess the positives and challenges of data collection and decide whether "value is added" to the jurisdiction's efforts to promote fair and impartial policing. The realities of social science should be considered in this decision-making, but so, too, should be the factors, independent of social science, that weigh in favor of or against measurement. *The key is making a fully informed decision.*

Outreach to Diverse Communities

Outreach to its diverse communities is an important part of an agency's efforts to produce fair and impartial policing. These "diverse communities" might reflect diversity based on race, ethnicity, national origin, age, sexual orientation, gender identity, immigration status, and/or other factors. This outreach can enhance trust and confidence and thereby advance the agency's legitimacy (Tyler 2004; Tyler et al. 2015), and can reduce perceptions of biased policing. The second desired outcome may be strongly related to the first. It is likely that a community member who has trust and confidence in a police department is less likely to interpret an interaction with a member of that department in a negative way (e.g., perceive biased policing).

First and foremost, developing strong relationships with the community starts with each and every contact an officer has with a community member, and we return to this important topic below. Additionally, though, many agencies have adopted programs and policies to outreach to diverse communities. Such programs are not new to law enforcement and therefore they do not need extensive coverage here.[44] Instead, a selection of outreach efforts from around the nation are reviewed. For instance, a number of agencies around the country have adopted "Coffee with a Cop." Case in point, the Omaha Police Department advertises ahead of time when and where officers will be having coffee. Sometimes community members show up to interact with the officers, but if they do not the officers ask individuals already in the establishment if they can sit down and chat with them. An article in the COPS Office e-newsletter "Dispatch," gives credit for the first such event to the

---

[44]Among many resources on this topic are *Building Relationships of Trust: Moving to Implementation* (Wasserman and Ginsburg 2014), *National Policy Summit on Community-Police Relations: Advancing a Culture of Community Cohesion and Trust* (IACP 2015), *Engaging Police in Immigrant Communities: Promising Practices from the Field* (Saint-Fort et al. 2012), *Strengthening Police-Community Relations in America's Cities: A Report of the US Conference of Mayors Working Group of Mayors and Police Chiefs* (U.S. Conference of Mayors 2015), *Final Report of the President's Task Force on 21st Century Policing* (President's Task Force on Twenty-First Century Policing 2015).

Hawthorne (CA) Police Department and reports that "over 175 communities across the nation" have implemented this outreach mechanism (Office of Community Oriented Policing Services 2013). In partnership with the Hawthorne P.D. and the University of Illinois Center for Public Safety and Justice, the COPS Office has instituted a national training program.[45]

The Minneapolis P.D. program "cops out of cars," conveys the direction to police personnel to emerge from their vehicles during their shifts and have proactive, positive contacts with community members. This goes hand in hand with long-term assignments of officers to neighborhoods so that relationships can develop. Similarly, soon after Anthony Holloway joined the St. Petersburg P.D. as chief in 2014, he initiated "Park, Walk and Talk." Pursuant to this initiative, all uniformed personnel, including the chief himself, must walk around a patrol area for at least an hour each week.

It was a community member in Yonkers who created "stop-and-shake." Business owner Hector Santiago came up with the idea of encouraging community members to approach a cop on the street, shake his or her hand and introduce themselves. Captain John Mueller with Yonkers P.D. reports, "The first step is the stop, then the shake, and then it's a conversation. And then it's getting to know each other on a very personal level .... And then all of a sudden, whatever stereotypes people have pent up inside, it kind of goes away. Because now you're looking at the person."[46]

Many agencies have Community Police Academies wherein community members are involved in a "course of study" to learn about policing.[47] For instance, the Bellefontaine P.D. (Ohio) initiated such a program in 2012. Their courses include a building tour and coverage of topics such as the history of policing, drug investigations, traffic enforcement, firearms safety and training, corrections, distracted driving, OVI enforcement, 911 dispatching, bike patrol and auxiliary units (Burger 2014). Many agencies put their participants through "shoot, don't shoot" video scenarios and have them ride along with officers.[48] Bellefontaine's Chief Standley reported that, "instating the CPA was a huge hit with the town, and an important part of helping citizens understand the roles of police" (Burger 2014).

Some departments have instituted engagement coordinators and/or teams—targeting specific communities. Minneapolis P.D. has a grant-funded Community Engagement Coordinator and a Community Engagement Team. The latter entity is

---

[45]There is a Coffee with a Cop Facebook page. Additionally, there is a website at www.coffeewithacop.com that provides downloadable resources for law enforcement agencies and allows agencies to post their events.

[46]At http://www.npr.org/blogs/codeswitch/2015/02/19/387479647/after-his-speech-on-race-and-police-complicated-feelings-in-comeys-hometown on 4/1/2015.

[47]Often these are labeled "Citizens' Police Academies." But the Seattle PD uses the label, "Community Police Academy." The term "community" is arguably superior to the term "citizens," because the latter is a legal term that would seem to imply that non-citizens are excluded by design.

[48]One of my own PhD students, Tom Jordan, evaluated a Citizens' Police Academy (CPA) as his dissertation research and found that the ride-along had the most impact of all of the CPA components in terms of improving attitudes toward police. See Jordan (1998).

designed to "better connect" MPD with its communities, including immigrant communities. Specific Engagement Team members liaison with the East African, Latino, Southeast Asian, African American, and Native American communities.

The Seattle Police Department has longstanding Demographic Advisory Councils comprised of community members. According to the Seattle.gov website, "These diverse councils provide an effective way to build bridges between minority communities and the police department, which results in increased awareness, improved understanding, and open dialogue regarding challenging issues including perceptions of racial profiling."[49] The councils support two-way dialogue, relationship building and mutual education. The specific councils are as follows:

- African American
- East African
- Filipino
- Korean
- Latino
- LGBTQ
- Muslim, Sikh, and Arab
- Native American
- South East Asian
- City-Wide Advisory Council.

Each council is formally linked to a member of the department's command staff and also supported by an officer liaison who attends meetings, educates the members about the department, responds to crisis situations, and otherwise facilitates police and community interaction.

The demographic advisory boards of the Hillsborough County (FL) Sheriff's Office have an important role in enhancing communication and understanding as pertains to police use of force. A representative from each of the Black and Hispanic Advisory Councils is invited to sit in on the Shooting Review Board meetings. They are encouraged to ask questions and are given the entire set of facts surrounding each incident. These individuals are not voting members, but are able to see the nature and depth of the review process. The expectation is that they will share their observations with other members of their communities and that this will reduce mistrust around this volatile national issue.

Much agency outreach has focused on communities defined by race, ethnicity or nationality. Many agencies outreach to other types of "diverse communities," such as those defined by sexual orientation, gender identity, and age. Immigrant communities, too, can be an important target of outreach efforts by police departments. The agencies involved with the Eagle County Law Enforcement Immigrant Advisory Council won two awards from the international Association of Chiefs of Police (IACP) in 2013—a Civil Rights award and a Community Policing award. Programs sponsored by the Council include "volunteer interpreters, coat and food

---

[49]http://www.seattle.gov/police/programs/advisory/.

drives, distribution of a frequently asked questions booklet, various outreach events, training for officers and the immigrant community, and a .... Spanish-based Citizens' Police Academy ..."[50] The program leaders credit the advisory council activities for the increased number of crimes reported by members of immigrant communities and a reduction in their victimization.[51] For some agencies, developing a trusting relationship between the police and immigrants is not about a "program," per se, but rather a decision not to enforce federal immigration laws when it comes to nonviolent offenders. All of the major Chiefs' organizations have highlighted the potential breech in trust and confidence on the part of undocumented communities when local police enforce federal immigration law. For instance, the Major City Chiefs Association in a position paper (2011) wrote that local law enforcement involvement in enforcement "undermines the trust and cooperation with the immigrant communities which are essential elements of community policing." (See also these documents produced by PERF, the Police Foundation, and IACP, respectively: Hoffmaster et al. 2010; PERF 2012; Khashu 2009; IACP 2006).

Programs reflecting outreach to LGBTQ communities are found across the country. The factors that have led the police to implement, or the community to call for, such initiatives include the tumultuous history of relationships between police and members of the LGBTQ communities (including large scale arrest of gay bar patrons in the 1950s and 1960s), and efforts to protect this community from hate crimes.

Some agencies, such as the Tampa P.D., NYPD, the Atlanta P.D., and the Washington Metropolitan P.D. (District of Columbia) have officers or units of officers that serve the LGBTQ outreach function and sometimes an investigative function as well (e.g., to investigate hate crimes). For instance, the NYPD has a Community Affairs LGBT Liaison Unit, which has the following responsibilities:

- Fostering positive relations between the LGBT community and the NYPD by providing a liaison for community members who may be crime victims, have information or issues of concern to the police department.
- Working with precincts, police (housing) service areas, and transit districts, located in areas with a large, visible LGBT community within them, to address concerns of that area.
- Assisting with productive dialogue with investigative units concerning LGBT related crimes.
- Working in partnership with other city agencies, other law enforcement entities, and community-based organizations, by conducting community outreach, education, and involvement in other LGBT related issues.
- Maintaining an interactive role in recruit based and in-service police trainings regarding the LGBT community.

---

[50]http://www.vailgov.com/release.asp?r_id=7989&type=#.

[51]For more examples of outreach to immigrant communities, see Saint-Fort et al. (2012), *Engaging Police in Immigrant Communities*.

- Conducting other various duties within Community Affaires as required.[52]

Another option is for the agency (e.g., Palm Springs, Baltimore P.D., and the Toronto Police Service) to form committees or councils that are comprised of *both* sworn personnel and LGBTQ community representatives. These committees can serve multiple functions, including those outlined by the Toronto Police Service (in describing the role of all of their Community Advisory Councils):

"To work together in partnership with identified community representatives in identifying, prioritizing, and problem-solving of policing issues by:

- Being proactive in community relations, crime prevention, education, mobilization, and communications initiatives
- Acting as a resource to the police and the community, and
- Developing a strategic long-term vision through building knowledge, education, tolerance and understanding."[53]

The Toronto LGBT Community Consultative Committee (CCC) holds monthly meetings and provides the LGBT community members with a direct line of communication to the chief. This CCC has organized a hate crime awareness program, has regular "Coffee with COPS" that target LGBT community members, and raises money to provide LGBT youth with scholarships to support their education. As of this writing, the TPS is engaging in focused outreach efforts to the transcommunity because, historically, a breech between the police service and this community has kept community members from reporting hate crimes against them.[54, 55]

Programs and Practices Directed at Youths

There are a number of policies and programs nationwide that reflect outreach to youths. These can serve to produce positive attitudes toward the police and maybe even plant the idea of a police career in young people. Referenced above were the various demographic advisory boards that some cities have established. In the same vein, to strengthen the relationship between the agency and youth, the Richmond (VA) P.D. formed the Young Adult Police Commissioners (YAPC),[56] which is

---

[52]http://www.nyc.gov/html/nypd/downloads/pdf/community_affairs/LGBTOutreach.pdf.

[53]http://www.torontopolice.on.ca/community/ccc.php.

[54]The Ontario Association of Chiefs of Police published in 2013 "Best Practices in Policing and LGBTQ Communities in Ontario" that was available (on 2/6/2015) at http://www.oacp.on.ca/Userfiles/Files/NewAndEvents/OACP%20LGBTQ%20final%20Nov2013.pdf. This document covers community engagement, recruitment and retention, and providing internal agency support for LGBTQ individuals.

[55]The St. Petersburg PD adopted a policy on police interactions with members of the transcommunity. Found on 9/29/2015 at http://static1.squarespace.com/static/54722818e4b0b3ef26cdc085/t/55f5e02de4b0f8a62c1244a4/1442177069212/Transgender+policy_St+Pete+PD+2015.pdf.

[56]Similarly Minneapolis developed a "Juvenile Outreach and Diversion" unit in 2013.

made up of juniors and seniors from all of the local high schools. According to the web site, "The focus of the Young Adult Police Commission is to give a voice to the youth of the city about issues that affect them and provide opportunities for youth to partner with police on problem solving strategies and discuss policing in general to give them a better understanding of what the police department does."[57]

Many agencies use School Resource Officers (SROs) to enhance the police-youth relationship. For instance, Chief Standley of the Bellefontaine (OH) P.D. recognized the potential of a school-based officer for improving youth attitudes toward police. He convinced the Town Council to fund a single officer who was to teach DARE and otherwise form relationships with the school kids. Officer Andy Kennedy, the first person in the position, reported, "Within weeks of starting the program, I went from having these kids looking at me in strange ways, wondering what an officer was doing in school, to having them greet me and smile when they saw me. I really saw those relationships begin to evolve with students of all ages."[58] Of course, not all SRO programs are geared toward (nor capable of) improving youths' attitudes toward the police. Programs that prioritize arrests for even low-level crimes and/or serve to replace what used to be teacher-imposed discipline, can have the opposite impact on the youths that, arguably, the police most need to reach.

The Milwaukee P.D. partnered with the Boys and Girls Club to develop the Students Talking it Over with Police or "STOP" program.[59] Trained officers meet with students for one hour every week for seven weeks in the school to teach youths about what police do and why. The purpose is to enhance youths' understanding of the police and improve attitudes. An experimental evaluation of the program showed positive impacts in terms of all objectives, including youth knowledge of police practices, general perceptions of police, and willingness to cooperate with police (Freiburger et al. 2015). Also bringing police and youth together in a classroom setting is the TAPS Academy (which stands for "Teen and Police Service") that has been implemented in a number of localities nationwide. According to the website, the TAPS Academy "is an 11-week program primarily designed for at-risk youth where students partner with mentor officers to discuss issues including bullying, anger management, avoidance of gang life, drug usage and conflict management, as well as other youth and law enforcement-focused topics."[60]

Another increasingly popular program is "Shop with a Cop." Pursuant to this program, local retailers agree to donate the goods that a low-income youth and a law enforcement officer select during a shopping spree for gifts for the youths' family members.

---

[57]http://www.richmondgov.com/police/YoungAdultPoliceCommissioners.aspx.

[58]This information and the quote come from an article in PoliceOne.com found on 9/29/2015 at http://www.policeone.com/chiefs-sheriffs/articles/7474149-RISE-Award-Nominee-3-ways-an-Ohio-PD-gained-their-communitys-trust/.

[59]www.stopbash.com.

[60]www.tapsacademy.org.

Again, the list of programs and potential programs is endless. Sarasota's Chief DiPino invites resident families to watch with police personnel a movie that is projected on the side of the department headquarters. In Boston during the summer months, an ice cream truck that is also a police cruiser, gives away ice cream to youths in high crime, low-income neighborhoods. The Kalamazoo P.D hosts block parties and holds a residential youth academy during the summer. The Rocky Mount (NC) P.D. (RMPD) joins with the city Parks and Recreation Department (PRD) to host "Summer Nights"; during weekends in July and August the RMPD and PRD host various activities to reduce idle time on the part of youths and allow youths to interact in a positive context with police personnel. The Tampa P.D. (TPD) sponsors a camp for youths that focuses on drug and alcohol prevention, gang suppression, and team building.[61] There is a TPD Police Athletic League or "PAL." The mission of this program, which has been adopted by many police agencies nationwide, is to use sports activities to build the bond between police and youths and prevent youth crime.[62] And, TPD has a youth leadership program called the "Training, Achievement and Confidence (TAC) Students Program."[63] Members of the Tactical Apprehension and Control Unit (also, not coincidentally "TAC") and others within the department provide instruction to teenagers to enhance decision making, planning, leadership, and relationship building.

There are Dragon Boat competitions all over the country, and the Orlando P.D. developed the first team in the nation that was comprised of police and high-risk youths. In its fourth year, the program now fields two teams of 20 that compete as the "Dueling Dragons of Orlando Dragon Boat Teams."[64]

Contact Theory Revisited

The programs and practices above serve a number of objectives—such as reducing crime, strengthening police-community relations, enhancing understanding of the police—and they can also serve to reduce bias through the power of the contact theory. In Chap. 2, the contact theory was described as a way that law enforcement officers could reduce their own biases—through positive contact with people who are different from themselves. These same positive interactions have the potential to reduce stereotypes about and biases against the police. When police are "ambiguous stimuli" on the streets of the city, people will "fill them in" with stereotypes about police. Of course, some will have positive stereotypes about police, but certain segments of the population are more likely to have negative stereotypes. When those individuals have the opportunity to interact in a *positive* context with

---

[61]http://tpdrichhouse.weebly.com/events.html.

[62]http://nationalpal.org/.

[63]http://www.talgov.com/tpd/tpd-tac-students.aspx.

[64]http://www.duelingdragonsorlando.com/.

individual officers—such as through the many programs described in this section—the contact theory predicts that this can reduce biases against, and stereotyping of, the police.

Recall, too, that the contact theory is strengthened when certain "favorable conditions" exist, such as (1) the individuals are working cooperatively to achieve a common goal, and (2) the two parties are interacting with equal status. As an example, these favorable conditions can be seen in the Orlando Dragon Boat Teams. First of all, the police and kids are working toward winning Dragon Boat competitions, which requires a team effort and maximum participant coordination. Second, the program organizer shared that, in the boat, the kids are encouraged to call the officers by their first names. This suggests that, in the boat, the rowers are equal partners with no status differential.

The section above highlights just a few of the many projects and programs that agencies have implemented all over North America to develop trust and confidence on the part of community members. It is important that these efforts involve agency officers broadly, instead of assigning this outreach to just a unit or a few. And, as previewed above, arguably more important that any agency program are the everyday interactions on the streets between line personnel and community members. Those interactions, if implemented consistent with the elements of procedural justice and with the attitude of a Guardian (not a Warrior), can reap volumes in trust, confidence, and thus, agency legitimacy (Elliott et al. 2011; Mazerolle et al. 2013; Sunshine and Tyler 2003; Tyler 2004).[65] These topics are covered in the section on Operations below.

Measuring Community Outreach

To quote Ron Davis, formerly the Chief in East Palo Alto and currently the Director of the COPS Office, "you get what you measure." That was the thinking of Captain Anthony Raimondo of Sanford, Florida. After the Trayvon Martin incident, the agency sought to strengthen its relationship with the community. Encouraging officers to engage with community members was accompanied by new *measures of productivity*. In addition to the "usual measures," such as "dispatched calls," "vehicle stops," and "crash report, other clearance," Sanford P.D. added "community outreach."[66] Under the heading of "community outreach" are the following subcategories:

---

[65]There is increasing recognition, too, of the importance and value of procedural justice *within* police agencies.

[66]Similarly, the Palo Alto (CA) P.D. established a call sign linked to various community outreach activities. This allows the agency to track these activities (at the individual, unit and agency levels), along with arrests, traffic tickets, field interrogation cards, and so forth (S. Brown, personal communication, 25 May 2015).

- Walk and talks
- Meetings and events
- Business contacts
- Mobile gym
- Other.

In the first month of implementation, there were 55 formally documented acts of outreach. In the second month, these almost doubled to 96. Captain Raimondo points out that "at this pace, we should document 1000 formal acts of community outreach in 2015" (personal communication, 16 March 2015).[67] Importantly, "those officers engaging in such activity get as much credit for the outreach as with criminal enforcement." And because productivity is assessed at the squad level, too, members of the squad can contribute to overall squad productivity, doing the policing that reflects their personal style. Officers who want to be crime fighters can emphasize that aspect of police work; officers who want to engage in outreach can spend time on that activity. Raimondo reports that officers appear happier because they are policing according to their own style. This is reflected in overall increased productivity, as confirmed by the fact that the "crime fighting" activities have not decreased with the additional outreach activities and measures. Raimondo reports that his next step is to "tighten up" what is defined as community outreach to make sure that the counted contacts are "meaningful."

Operations to Promote Bias-Free Policing and the Perceptions of it

Agency leaders need to ensure that their operations promote both fair and impartial policing and the perceptions of it on the part of community members. This is a broad directive, since it encompasses much of what the police department is doing on the streets of the jurisdiction, including the nature and tone of the agency's interactions with community members. Although broad, it can be boiled down to four directives:

- Give serious consideration to complaints of operational bias
- Reduce the risk of bias in high-discretion, crime-control-focused activities
- Adopt policing models that promote bias-free policing and the perceptions of it
- Avoid profiling by proxy.

---

[67]Raimondo is encouraging officers to take photographs of the outreach to produce a visual library of the department's focus on positive relationships with community members.

Take Seriously Community Complaints of Operational Bias

Many complaints of bias reflect a concern about the actions of an individual officer. In contrast, a complaint of "operational bias" reflects concern about a department's policies or practices. As examples, the complaint in Chicago from community members was that the locations of seatbelt checkpoints were selected to target low-income, African-American neighborhoods. In Seattle, the alleged bias was in the targeting of downtown, open-air drug markets for enforcement, instead of attending to the drug use and dealing that occurred inside the homes of the economically advantaged. In Austin and Fayetteville, the concern was that racial/ethnic minorities were targeted for requests for consent searches. In Tampa, the concerns were with bike stops, and the NYPD has been criticized for alleged bias in its use of stop and frisk. The key objective here is for the leader of an agency to be ready and willing to take such complaints seriously, instead of dismissing them in a knee-jerk reaction. Knowing what we now know about how bias manifests in even well-intentioned individuals, and because we have humans in policy-making positions within the departments, a police leader must acknowledge the possibility that an agency's practices could reflect or promote bias—even if wholly unintentional.

When a complaint of operational bias is raised, the agency's first step is to conduct an investigation. Often, although not always, data can be brought to bear. Can seatbelt checkpoint locations be justified by crash data? Can a focus on open-air drug markets be justified by the documented harms associated with such drug dealing and calls for service that are not matched in high-income residential areas? Can claims of overdeployment or underdeployment be refuted by call-for-service data?

As an example, a common complaint in big cities is differential enforcement at clientele-specific bars. Maybe the claim is that the bars frequented by the LGBTQ community or by racial/ethnic minorities receive more aggressive enforcement than do the bars frequented by heterosexuals or Caucasians. An agency informed of such concerns would want to assess (a) whether the enforcement at the bars was different, and (b) if it was, whether there was a justification for this differential enforcement. Assessing the first could call upon police activity data, such as for vehicle and pedestrian stops, arrests, and searches. If this assessment indicated differential enforcement, the next step would be to examine other data to see if it was justified or not. In this assessment, the key questions are whether there is different behavior on the part of patrons and/or different responses to bar behavior on the part of bar owners and/or neighbors. Importantly, to examine the behavior of bar patrons, the agency cannot consider its own activity records. That there are more stops and/or arrests at one bar compared to the other could merely reflect biased enforcement and not differential patron behavior. So agencies would want to focus on data that is independent of enforcement, such as calls for service and reports of crime. There might also be stationary videos that could be used as a resource and/or agency employees could conduct observations.

Of course, if an agency finds differential enforcement and no justification for it, the practices need to be revised and the officers involved would be counseled or disciplined as appropriate. But, even if an agency concludes, after a serious and genuine investigation, that the practices are bias-free, its work is not done.[68] Agency representatives would return to the complainants (e.g., the bar owner or organized group) and share the results of the analysis. The communication would be that the agency (1) took the complaint seriously, (2) researched it, and (3) produced the following findings indicating bias-free enforcement. Then, in the vein of problem-solving, that agency might work with the relevant stakeholders to reduce the issues that produce the agency enforcement activities.

As above, an agency is not done even after concluding that a practice is bias free. In some situations, it may be that the perceptions of bias surrounding the practice are (1) not allayed by the "investigation" and communication outlined above, and/or (2) otherwise producing a big "hit" to the agency in terms of community member attitudes toward the department. In such a case it will be constructive to ask: *Does this practice produce sufficient crime control benefit to offset the harm done to trust and legitimacy?* This was the question for Chief Knee in Austin back in 2010, when he faced allegations that requests for consent to search were targeted toward racial/ethnic minorities. Chief Knee did not find evidence that the requests were biased,[69] but it became clear that the concerns were strong and unabated by his investigation and "results." He explored the efficacy of those consent searches by looking at the hit rate. If an agency determined that 20 % of the consent searches were turning up seizable evidence such as guns and drugs, then that agency might decide that the crime control value was significant and retain the practice—hopefully working in other ways to strengthen trust and confidence. Chief Knee, however, found that the hit rate for the consent searches was very low; he determined that the crime control value of the practice was not sufficient to outweigh the harm to trust and confidence. What might an agency leader, such as Knee, do in this situation? Implementing steps to enhance the crime control value of the practice can reduce the frequency and increase the effectiveness of the activity; these steps could at least reduce the *number* of negative contacts with the aggrieved group and likely eliminate the most *arbitrary* (and, therefore, possibly biased) of these contacts. [This type of intervention is consistent with NYPD Commissioner Bratton's statement in March of 2015, in the context of the stop and frisk discussion, wherein he reported that NYPD will, in 2015, have a million fewer law enforcement contacts with community members. Bratton reported: "I'm not interested in quantity. I'm interested in quality" (Parascandola et al. 2015).] Regarding consent searches, a chief or sheriff might decide (as some have) to require articulable suspicion for a

---

[68]And importantly, as discussed above, it is very difficult to measure biased policing and so the results of these investigations should not be considered conclusive proof of either biased practices or bias-free practices.

[69]It is difficult to determine whether consent searches are biased. It's easy to determine if there is disparity in their implementation, but challenging to determine whether that disparity is justified or not. See Fridell (2004).

consent search and require a consent form to be signed by the subject. Also, importantly, one could implement training on the science of implicit bias because, as highlighted below, high-discretion, crime-control-focused activities are at particular risk of bias. The goals of these efforts might be to increase the hit rates over time and mend the breach in community–police relations.[70]

Reduce the Risk of Bias in High-Discretion, Crime-Control-Focused Activities

To produce fair and impartial policing and the perceptions of it, police leaders need to understand the high risk of bias associated with high-discretion, crime-control-focused activities and take steps to reduce that risk. The point that high-discretion activities pose a particular risk of biased policing was raised in Chap. 2 of the book in discussing how implicit bias might manifest in policing. I presented the example of an agency that directed its personnel to engage in frequent consensual encounters and to collect information from the person (that is, the officers filled out what are commonly referred to as "contact cards" or "field interrogation cards"). The personnel were given no particular instructions as to whom to target, but were told that the information they collected would be important for crime control. The point made before and reiterated here is that, barring any direction to the contrary, officers told to engage in some high-discretion activity geared toward preventing or solving crimes will, says the science, default to the demographic groups they link through stereotypes to crime and violence.

Another example comes from a jurisdiction where the chief told his personnel "use your traffic-stop powers to find the guns, find the drugs." As police personnel will acknowledge, a cop can pull over pretty much any car she wants and meet the requirements of the 4th amendment; per conventional wisdom, it takes fewer than two minutes to identify a traffic violation on the part of any driver that would justify a stop.[71] So with this directive, the chief was instructing his personnel to target the cars that look like they have "bad guys" in them. Indeed, in describing this practice to me and others, he stated that "I don't expect them to be pulling over four nuns."

This chief's directive, that suggests that officers should target criminals for traffic stops, even when no indication of criminal behavior is required, begs the question: *on what basis will they target "the bad guys" if it is not crime-relevant behavior?* It is not far-fetched to suggest that demographics might enter into these selection

---

[70]Some personnel, particularly at the lowest levels, might find it "soft" to prioritize trust and legitimacy over crime control efforts. But, as discussed below, producing trust and legitimacy *is* a crime control endeavor.

[71]A stop can meet the 4th amendment and still be unconstitutional if the officer is violating the equal protection provision of the 14th amendment.

decisions. Well-intentioned officers might target individuals in the groups that are disproportionately involved in crime (e.g., youths, Blacks, men, low-income individuals), which means the officers are treating individuals within groups as if they match the group stereotype/characteristic. As argued above, this is biased policing. Recall the argument that, even if stereotypes are based in part on fact, we err when we treat members of the group as if they match the stereotype.[72]

Clearly, despite the risks for biased policing, we cannot do away with high-discretion police activities focused on crime control. And, indeed, we need not do so, but precautions must be taken. First, the agency must educate personnel on how their implicit biases put them at risk for biased policing in such circumstances and also give them skills for implementing these types of directives in a fair and impartial policing manner. (See section on training above.) Personnel need to understand how human biases might lead them to interpret the same behavior (e.g., "furtive actions") on the part of two groups differently.[73] Recognizing the risk of bias associated with a high-discretion program, the Boston P.D. determined that they wanted implicit bias training for their personnel *before* implementing Data-Driven Approaches to Crime and Traffic Safety (DDACTS). DDACTS "integrates location-based traffic crash, crime, and calls for service and enforcement data to establish effective and efficient methods for deploying law enforcement resources" (National Highway Traffic Safety Administration 2014, p. ii). If implemented in accordance with guidelines, there is little danger of bias in terms of the selection of geographic areas to receive attention; but, to avoid bias at the officer-implementation level, DDACTS agencies need to attend to the directions they give officers assigned to these areas; they need to make sure the directives do not sound like "use your traffic stop capabilities to find the guns, find the drugs."[74]

As a second precaution to reduce the risk of bias in high-discretion police activities that are focused on crime control, agencies need to stop what Susan Herman, the NYPD Deputy Commissioner for Collaborative Policing, calls "unfocused, massive enforcement efforts" (Obbie 2015). These unfocused activities produce a risk of biased application—where the targets become *populations* and not *behavior*. [According to Obbie (2015), Bratton appointed Herman to replace "brute crime suppression" with "racially sensitive crime prevention."] And, indeed, the

---

[72]Recall, that according to the "Second Circle" definition of biased policing, there is a point at which "disproportional involvement" might become actionable intelligence.

[73]Such training can acknowledge that sometimes behavior *does* mean different things within different cultures/groups. In one culture, lack of eye contact may indicate deception, in another it might indicate respect.

[74]Bias-promoting "operational directives" might come in the form of measurement. As the saying goes, "You get what you measure" (or, similarly, "you get what you coach"). So, if an agency is measuring or otherwise reinforcing number of searches and pounds of marijuana seized, it could, unwittingly promote *quantity* of interventions and raise the risk of bias; to remedy, the agency might instead promote *quality* of encounters by measuring search hit rates.

controversy involving the NYPD use of stop and frisk is relevant here.[75, 76, 77] Other examples of high-discretion, crime control-focused activities that have raised concerns include the "cold consent encounters" used by the Drug Enforcement Administration, public housing patrols in NYC, low-level marijuana arrests, and "Zero Tolerance" policing.[78] And, for any of these, the bias may not manifest just in the *individuals* who are selected for enforcement, but in the *geographic locations* selected for these operations. An example allegation of "geographic bias" came from a report submitted to city government officials by the Police Complaints Board (PCB) in Washington DC (District of Columbia Police Complaints Board 2013). The concern was with the potentially race-biased enforcement of the automobile window tint laws. The Metropolitan DC Police Department (MPD) had responded to these concerns by arguing that the selection of individuals for tinted windows could not be biased because officers cannot see who is driving the car. The PCB wrote: "… racial profiling in this context is not necessarily limited to an officer's ability to assess a motorist visually; instead, it could be evidenced by a geographic disparity in enforcement. (Complaint data) indicates that MPD may be focusing enforcement of the window tint law in areas populated by people of color."

Instead of "brute crime suppression" (Obbie 2015), police need to adopt focused, information-led strategies that target behaviors and not populations, and those strategies should be adopted with the cooperation and support of community members as discussed below.

Adopt Policing Models that Promote Bias-Free Policing and the Perceptions of it

Law enforcement agencies should implement models of policing that support fair and impartial policing and the perceptions of it. So what does that policing look

---

[75]The Urban Institute and COPS Office produced a document characterizing the NYPD practice and the potential harms of it, including the potential for biased application (LaVigne et al. 2014). The authors distinguish between traditional stop and frisk and the NYPD application of it, which they characterized as an "intense crime deterrence strategy." Fourth and fourteenth amendment concerns were raised; regarding the latter, LaVigne et al. (2014, p. 5) wrote: "By targeting specific communities through stop and frisk tactics, stop and frisk can lend itself to discriminatory—and unconstitutional—policing that is reliant on profiling and stereotyping."

[76]Recall, District Court Judge Shira A. Scheindlin, when reflecting on the NYPD stop and frisk practices of the NYPD suggested that "unconscious biases" might explain some of the police behaviors that she deemed constitutional violations (*Floyd vs. City of New York*).

[77]See Epp et al. (2014) for an insightful analysis of how investigative stops "undermine racial equality and democratic values".

[78]I intentionally do not include "Broken Windows" policing on this list. I believe this term has been used—by community groups and even police—to describe activities that were never a part of the original conceptualization of Broken Windows Theory as outlined in Wilson and Kelling (1982). This term is often inappropriately used to describe activities more appropriately linked to "Zero Tolerance Policing." See Kelling (2015), and White et al. (2015).

like? Lum and Nagin (2015) developed a "7-point blueprint for the 21st century"—arguing that police need to prioritize *both* (1) crime prevention *and* (2) promoting police legitimacy. Their plan has implications for promoting fair and impartial policing and the perceptions of it. The two authors point out that police will not be able to "arrest (their) way out of crime" (p. 2). Arrest highlights the failure of prevention and a policing model that makes arrest the top priority is more likely than other models to alienate significant communities. The communities "at the receiving end" of arrest-focused policing are likely to be the same ones that perceive biased enforcement (e.g., communities of color, low-income neighborhoods, youths), and, indeed, time and time again, we have seen community alienation articulated in terms of "police targeting" and "bias." Lum and Nagin (2015) caution against "zero tolerance"; aggressive, deterrence-focused stop and frisk; and Broken Windows "as it is commonly practiced"[79] They advocate replacing these tactics with others that can both reduce crime and improve police legitimacy. Consistent with such a blueprint are many well-known police strategies, including:

- Crime prevention efforts that are focused on the highest risk places and people and that use circumstance-specific problem-solving approaches (Lum and Nagin 2015),[80]
- Community policing
- Training and policies that promote de-escalation
- Alternatives to Arrest[81]
- Policing that reflects the principles of procedural justice
- Policing in the vein of the Guardian, not the Warrior.

Most of these concepts are far from new and are thus well known in policing. The last two listed—procedural justice and Guardian versus Warrior—are receiving much attention in contemporary discussions of policing and so are discussed below.

Procedural Justice

The concept of "procedural justice" was referenced above; Tom Tyler has been instrumental in linking this concept to policing and the achievement of police legitimacy (Sunshine and Tyler 2003; Tyler 2004; Tyler et al. 2015; see also Elliott et al. 2011). Procedural justice reflects the fact that, when individuals look back on their encounters with police, they do not focus just on the outcome of those encounters—for instance, whether they got a ticket or were arrested. They focus as

---

[79]As above, the term "Broken Windows" has been variously utilized. Here Lum and Nagin (2015) refer to the form whereby there are large numbers of arrests for minor crimes with an eye toward preventing more serious crime. As referenced above, this "common practice" is not fully consistent with the original formulation.

[80]Implemented right, these are the opposite of the "unfocused, massive enforcement efforts" referenced above.

[81]Including, for instance, civil citation programs and other diversion efforts. See Frost (2015).

much or more on *how they were treated.* Procedural justice highlights the importance of four characteristics of encounters: (1) respect,[82] (2) trustworthiness (e.g., conveying worthy intentions, caring), (3) voice (e.g., allowing a person to share their point of view), and (4) neutrality.[83] Tyler points out that procedural justice is a means for producing police legitimacy; that is, it can increase the extent to which community members accept the police as a legitimate authority. High perceptions of legitimacy can serve the police in a number of ways; for instance, community members who perceive the police as a legitimate authority may be more likely to assist the police in their crime control and other efforts (e.g., call the police when a crime occurs, provide information on a crime being investigated, attend community meetings with police, join neighborhood watch) and are even more likely to obey the law (see e.g., Tyler 2006; Elliott et al. 2011). This assistance can help the police reduce crime and disorder.

"Guardian Versus Warrior" Mentality in Policing

Walker (2015, p. 1) calls the debate about whether the Warrior or Guardian mentality should prevail as "the war for the soul of American policing." Stoughton (2015), a former copturned law professor, argues that the Warrior mindset hinders "efforts to improve public perceptions of police legitimacy" and, instead, he extolls the virtues of the Guardian mentality for modern policing. The Warrior mindset, according to Stoughton, is produced when police are trained that they face "an intensely hostile world" and are in combat with the individuals they are sworn to protect and serve (p. 227). As Chief Cathy Lanier of the Metropolitan Police Department in Washington DC reported (Williams 2015), "We tell these kids when they come out of the academy, 'Everyone is trying to kill you.'" This mindset affects how officers interact with community members and hinders relationship building.

It is easy to see how a Warrior mindset can exacerbate tensions between the police and communities that already have strained relationships with police—for instance, men of color in low-income neighborhoods. The Warrior officer may enter into encounters with low income, Black males with a mindset of control and an expectation of lack of deference on the part of the subject; the Warrior mindset will produce a manner of entry into the encounter that could actually *produce* the lack of deference that the officer anticipated, and then the situation could easily spiral downward. Stoughton (2015, p. 229) describes the Warrior's approach and the consequences of it: "the assertive manner in which officers set the tone of an

---

[82]Treating people with dignity and respect has led to a question in policing: when, if ever, is it appropriate for police to use offensive language, such as in the form of profanity? See Baseheart and Cox (1993) for an assessment of the impact of police profanity on community members and commentary by Walker (2015).

[83]Several PERF documents provide practical information on the implementation and impact of procedural justice. See PERF (2014a, b).

encounter can also set the stage for a negative response or a violent interaction that was, from the start, avoidable."[84]

The Guardian mindset, on the other hand, reflects a commitment and priority to protect and serve.[85] According to Stoughton (2015: p. 21):

> Both Warriors and Guardians seek to protect the communities they serve ... but the guardian mindset takes both a broader view and a longer view of how to achieve that goal. Put simply, the guardian mindset prioritizes service over crime fighting, and it values the dynamics of short-term encounters as a way to create long-term relationships. As a result, it instructs officers that their interactions with community members must be more than legally justified, they must also be empowering, fair, respectful, and considerate. The guardian mindset emphasizes communication over commands, cooperation over compliance, and legitimacy over authority.

Abusive Policing

Where does abusive policing fit into the discussion of operations to promote fair and impartial policing and the perceptions of it?[86] A police officer who engages in abusive policing is very likely practicing biased policing. It just makes sense that abusive policing is inherently biased.[87] An abusive officer is unlikely to be abusive toward a person who appears to have power; an officer would be concerned that such a person would have the means (and credibility) to expose the officer's misconduct and hold him to account. Instead, an officer would engage in abusive policing with individuals who seem not to have the means to bring him to account. As a White woman, often in professional dress, driving a respectable car, I am unlikely to be (and indeed, have never been) on the receiving end of abusive, even unprofessional, policing. Instead, we hear the stories of abusive policing against the less powerful as might be defined in terms of race, age, undocumented status, socioeconomic status, and/or criminal record.[88]

---

[84]Rahr and Rice (2015) describe what academy training looks like that can produce the Guardian mindset. Other training programs consistent with fair, just and relationship-strengthening policing include Crisis Intervention Training, Strategies for Youth, and Blue Courage, to name a few.

[85]Some police argue that the Guardian sometimes needs to become the Warrior to, for instance, use force. This is a misunderstanding of the concepts as set forth in the literature. The Guardian has all of the tools that the Warrior has, including deadly force; it is the *attitude* that is different.

[86]"Abusive policing," as used here, encompasses a range of bad police behaviors ranging from disrespectful treatment of people to excessive use of force and other violations of the constitution and/or law.

[87]This has not been documented empirically. It is very difficult to measure biased policing and very difficult to measure abusive policing; it would be doubly difficult to measure the confluence of the two.

[88]And the same link between abusive policing and biased policing applies at the geographic level. To the extent that an agency culture supports abusive policing, again, it is unlikely to support such abuse against the powerful segments of the community; instead, the abuse will occur (and maybe

This link between abusive policing and the powerless was articulated well by a participant at a summit hosted by the International Association of Chiefs of Police in the wake of the Ferguson events.[89] In discussing how to improve community–police relations, many in the group—made up of police leaders and concerned community stakeholders (e.g., representatives from the Urban League and ACLU) —started to talk about a "whole new model of policing" that might be needed to strengthen police-community relations. One of the community stakeholders suggested that we do not need a new model of policing; instead, we need to implement with the *powerless* in society the same model of policing routinely used for the *powerful*.

The implication above is that mistreatment is targeted toward certain groups because of an officer's perception that these individuals cannot hold him or her to account for the abuse. But the research on implicit bias posits an additional mechanism that might explain why some groups are more likely than others to be on the receiving end of police abuse—dehumanization. As the term implies, "dehumanization" is when a person perceives another person or group of people as something less than human (see e.g., Goff et al. 2008 and Harris and Fiske 2011). Dehumanization is what Fiske found in the study mentioned in Chap. 2, in which she compared the brain activity of subjects (through magnetic resonance imaging) when they were shown pictures of people who looked homeless and when they were shown pictures of people who did not look homeless.[90] Imaging consistent with thinking about *people* was produced when the subjects saw the non-homeless pictures, but not when they saw the homeless photos. The brain activity for when the subjects saw photos of people who looked homeless was consistent with thoughts of disgust and avoidance. Harris and Fiske (2011), too, used MRI to document dehumanization and suggest that this mechanism could "explain the all-too-human ability to commit atrocities such as hate crimes, prisoner abuse, and genocide against people who are dehumanized." Goff et al. report:

> Dehumanization is viewed as a central component to intergroup violence because it is frequently the most important precursor to moral exclusion, the process by which stigmatized groups are placed 'outside the boundary in which moral values, rules, and considerations of fairness apply' (Opotow 1990, p. 1). Groups that are morally excluded do not count in a moral sense. Consequently, anything that is done to someone who is morally excluded is permissible, no matter how heinous the action (2008, 293).

In their study, Goff et al. found that their subjects dehumanized Blacks and they further found that this dehumanization of Blacks led to the "greater endorsement of violence [by police] against a Black suspect than against a White suspect." (p. 304).

(Footnote 88 continued)

even be condoned by the agency culture) in the parts of the jurisdiction where the least powerful live.

[89]The document that was produced based on this summit is IACP (2015).

[90]This study was introduced in Chap. 2 to show the automatic and physiological nature of implicit biases.

Abusive policing, whatever the mechanism producing it, can precipitate a downward spiral in the relationship between the police and the group that is abused, or that even *perceives* itself to be abused. If the police have been engaging in abusive policing (or even engaging in "heavy-handed" tactics) with a community, this can breed community distrust; these individuals on the receiving end of these tactics are therefore likely to bring less deference to an encounter with a police officer than would someone not similarly alienated. This reduced deference can lead to more abusive and/or heavy-handed tactics, and the spiral downward continues. The formula is:

- Abusive and/or heavy-handed tactics produces community distrust
- Community distrust produces less deference with police
- Less deference leads to abusive and/or heavy-handed tactics
- Repeat.

The key is to adopt policing models that "break the cycle of recrimination and distrust between communities and cops" (Obbie 2015), such as those discussed above.

Avoid Profiling by Proxy

In discussing how to use operations to promote both bias-free policing and the perceptions of it, we have discussed (a) taking serious the complaints of operational bias from community members; (b) reducing the risk of bias in high-discretion, crime-control activities; and (c) adopting policing models that promote fair and impartial policing and the perceptions of it. Finally, in thinking about operations, agency leaders need to consider the challenges posed by "profiling by proxy" and provide guidance to their employees regarding how they should handle such situations. As reported earlier, profiling by proxy occurs when a community member seeks police assistance because of his/her own biases. Shared earlier was the scenario wherein an elderly White female in a mostly White neighborhood calls the police because there is a "suspicious person out front." The only thing she can articulate is that it is a Black male in a car. She does not report any information that links the man to criminal activity. In a similar vein, profiling by proxy might come to the police as "three kids up to no good" on the corner, gay couples expressing affection, and/or Hispanic laborers "loitering" on a corner, to name a few examples.

There are powerful differences of opinions about how a police agency should react to such calls—as indicated by the conversations my fellow trainers and I have had around the country when discussing the "Black man in a car" scenario. In these discussions, trainees are asked to identify three ways to respond to this situation and the pros and cons of each.[91] One popular option is to have the officer respond to the car door of the man and implement a professional, consensual encounter. The positive aspects of this are that the caller will be pleased by this response, the officer might uncover criminal activity that is now thwarted by his presence, and the man in the car might need assistance or otherwise welcome the contact with the police. Negatives include the possibility that the officer is, in fact, engaging in biased policing—at the behest of a community member, and the possibility that the man in the car reacts very negatively to the encounter. Regarding the latter, some police in this discussion insist that "it's *all about* the professional manner or approach," when, in fact, even the most professional approach might produce an angry response; this might not be the first time (maybe even *this week*) that this Black man is approached by a smiling, professional officer to inquire as to why he is where he is. To paraphrase former Chief Michael Scott (personal communication, 14 February 2008), it might feel to the man in the car as if he's being asked to justify his existence on the White streets of America—and maybe he is. Many police professionals in this country proclaim vehemently that interacting with the man in the car is the *only* viable response and are even disbelieving when told that other police professionals around the country do not agree. They insist that they *must* respond to all calls for service (although sometimes they will acknowledge that "responding" to a call might not necessarily require approaching the Black man in the car).

At the other end of the continuum of possible responses, some professionals suggest that contact be made with the complainant (e.g., by phone) and questions asked to determine whether there is, in fact, indications of criminal activity that were not originally solicited by dispatch and/or conveyed by the complainant. If, after questioning, there is no evidence of criminal activity, these professionals indicate that they would *not* send an officer to the scene. For instance, a supervisor hearing this dispatch would be authorized in some departments to rescind the directive. Individuals proposing this response report that they would want to reinforce the caller nonetheless because, in many jurisdictions, we ask community members to call and report suspicious activity. So the supervisor might thank the woman for calling, explain why no officer would be coming to the scene, and encourage her to call again if she sees evidence of criminal activity.[92] The possible downsides of this response are an unhappy complainant and the possibility that criminal activity is, in fact, occurring and now continues unabated. The latter potential "con" is, of course particularly powerful, although others argue in response, that this is a frequent possibility in the policing world, but that police must act on the information that they *have* (after due diligence) and not on somewhat remote possibilities of what *might occur*. Relatedly, some agencies have

---

[91]The instructions vary by the subgroup being trained. For instance, patrol officers are asked about three options *they have* if dispatched to this call. Agency leaders are asked to identify three ways *an agency* might react to such circumstances.

[92]Some training participants have suggested that they might want to talk about implicit biases at, for instance, Neighborhood Watch meetings, to reduce "profiling by proxy."

finite resources and must therefore prioritize calls that reflect true criminal activity. The pros of not approaching the man are that the police have not engaged in biased policing on the basis of community members' stereotypes and do not risk the potential negative interaction with the man in the car, as described above.

An option in between those two ends of the continuum is to have a cop drive by to see for herself whether there are indications of criminal activity. This would likely be more welcome by the complainant than the "no police response" option described above. If there is no evidence of criminal activity, then there would be no need for the (potentially negative) interaction with the man in the car.

I am not suggesting that there is one "right" response, but am arguing that this is an important discussion for the police profession. It is important to reflect on this question: If, in fact, this woman is calling because she has a Black-crime implicit association (obviously, in the "real world" this is not always clear), is it acceptable for the police department to do her bidding? The rhetorical questions are these:

- If an officer went to the car door of the man based on his *own* Black-crime implicit association, would it be biased policing?
- If an officer went to the car door of the man based on his *sergeant's* Black-crime implicit association, would it be biased policing?
- If an officer went to the car door of the man based on the *community member's* Black-crime implicit association, would it be biased policing?

At the very least, police leaders need to provide guidance to their personnel about the agency's "preferred response."[93] The importance of this was highlighted by an experience of mine. In a training class for sergeants, I directed the attendees to "identify three responses to this (Black man in a car) scenario and the pros and cons of each." One of the trainees looked up at me with a perplexed expression: "Is this a trick question?" He asked that because, it turned out, his three responses would be (1) go to the car door of the man, (2) go to the car door of the man, and/or (3) go to the car door of the man. Two days later when I was having this same discussion with this sergeant's agency leadership, I learned that this was NOT the chief's preferred response. Instead, the chief favored the communications with the woman complainant and a rescinded dispatch by a supervisor if no criminal activity was indicated. This anecdote highlights the importance of having agency leadership communicating with personnel about how to handle "profiling by proxy" situations, although such communications will recognize that there is not one "cookie cutter response" for the infinite possible variations of "profiling by proxy."

---

[93]This might include training call-takers to ask important questions upon receipt of a call similar to "black man out front in a car."

Transforming the Richmond (CA) Police Department

This section on operations can be most effectively summarized with a success story. Chris Magnus, who served as chief of police in Richmond (CA) from 2005 to 2015, proved the value of strategic, focused operations (versus "brute crime suppression") and other measures to promote community trust, promote fair and impartial policing, *and* reduce crime.[94] In 2005, Richmond, which is a majority-minority city, had a history of high crime,[95] "enforcement driven" policing, and a strained relationship between the police and community members. Chief Magnus turned the city around with a number of initiatives.

Magnus expanded community policing from a handful of officers to agency-wide implementation. Everyone in the agency is charged with enhancing police-community trust. Patrol officers are given long-term assignments and are directed to develop police-community relationships in their areas. They are expected to be out of their cars interacting with community members, in churches, in businesses, in schools and at community meetings. These activities are recorded and personnel evaluations and career advancement are based in part on an officer's success at strengthening community relationships. Everyone is expected to engage in short-term and long-term problem solving. COMPSTAT meetings are not solely crime-focused; the discussions and reports address community engagement, community concerns and quality of life issues. Magnus had his personnel trained in Fair and Impartial Policing; procedural justice; "Tact, Tactics, and Trust: Tactical Human Dynamics"; "Policing the Teenage Brain"[96]; Crisis Intervention Training; and in other state-of-the-art topics.

Magnus moved the department away from the "enforcement-driven" policing. Soon after he arrived, he disbanded the "street teams." These teams were in the highest crime areas and, according to Magnus, "would roust anybody who's out walking around, with the idea that they might have a warrant outstanding or be holding drugs" (Murphy 2015). Magnus (personal communication, 22 February 2015) says these "fishing expeditions" were inefficient, ineffective, and served to alienate community members. According to Lt. Pickett: "We had generations of families raised to hate and fear the Richmond police, and a lot of that was the result of our style of policing in the past. It took us a long time to turn that around and we're seeing the fruits of that now. There is a mutual respect now, and some mutual compassion" (Elias 2015). The more positive views of police on the part of residents have been confirmed with community surveys (personal communication, 2 June 2015).

---

[94]This information comes from newspaper articles (Early 2014; Elias 2015; Murphy 2015; Rogers and DeBolt 2014; Romney 2015; Weise 2015), a personal interview with Chief Magnus on 2/22/2015, and personal correspondence (June 2015).

[95]In 2007, Richmond was the ninth-most dangerous city in the country per capita (Weise 2015).

[96]See also "Strategies for Youth" at http://strategiesforyouth.org/.

Crime is down significantly in Richmond (see e.g., Romney 2015; Elias 2015). For instance, in 2005, when Magnus joined the department, there were 40 murders in the city. They have been reduced every year up to 2014 during which there were 11 murders (Elias 2015). Magnus attributes this, in large part, to the enhanced trust and confidence in the department. Much more than before, community members come forward to report crimes and provide information to aid in investigations. Additionally, in Richmond, crime prevention and control is not the sole responsibility of the police department. There is a city-wide focus on violence as a public health epidemic and all city unit heads have a commitment to and a role in violence reduction.

Use of force, especially deadly force, is down in the RPD. This can be attributed to a clear message from the chief that force will be used as a last resort and scrutinized closely. Officers have been given Tasers and pepper spray and enhanced training on verbal de-escalation skills. Personnel receive *monthly* use-of-force training and, four times a year, they do role-playing on how to disarm suspects. Following his attendance at the Police Executive Research Forum program on "Re-Engineering Force" (PERF 2015), Magnus wrote in a newspaper opinion piece: "The Richmond Police Department trains its officers to appropriately assess risk, develop crisis resolution strategies reflecting best practices, and demonstrates flexibility responding to critical incidents (including the ability to tactically reposition or 'throttle back' certain actions to avoid encounters such as 'suicide by cop')." The strong message and training around force has produced results. RPD averaged less than 1 officer-involved shooting per year since 2008, and no one has been killed by a RPD officer since 2007 (Rogers and DeBolt 2014). This rate is lower than other law enforcement agencies in the region (Murphy 2015).[97] Of the over 3,000 arrests made by RPD officers in 2014, less than 6 % involved the use of force (Magnus 2015).

Magnus held personnel to account. As one newspaper article reported (Murphy 2015), "Magnus has demoted and fired more officers than two decades of previous chiefs combined." Body cameras, vehicle monitoring and an early intervention system support accountability.

As part of his overall efforts to promote fair and impartial policing and the perceptions of it, the chief made hiring decisions in a manner consistent with his vision. Upon his arrival, he made it a top priority to hire and promote more women, Asians, Latinos, and African Americans. (The department is approximately 40 % White and 60 % Black, Latino, Asian, and/or Native American.) He reports, "when you have a department that doesn't look anything like the community it serves, you're asking for trouble, no matter how dedicated and professional your employees are" (quoted in Early 2014). In terms of diversity hiring, he reports that "diversity" encompasses life experience such as growing up in Richmond or cities like Richmond. With his hiring, Magnus sought individuals "who are good listeners, who have patience, who don't feel that it takes away from their authority to demonstrate kindness" (Early 2014, p. 5).

---

[97]And, importantly, no officers were feloniously killed during Magnus' 10 years as chief.

Chapter 4
The Way Ahead

Chapter 2 of this book covered the science of bias and its application to policing and Chap. 3 described what police agencies can and should do to promote fair and impartial policing and the perceptions of it. For too long, police professionals, along with community stakeholders, have been working under the old paradigm; the belief has been that officers with explicit biases, and *only* officers with explicit biases, produce biased policing. Agency leaders have varied in the level of their efforts to reduce biased policing, but even the most dedicated leaders have been narrowly focused on rooting out, or at least holding to account, police with explicit biases. The new paradigm recognizes that there are individuals in policing with *explicit* biases, but also recognizes that even well-intentioned police professionals have biases—implicit biases—that can impact their perceptions and behavior.

As mentioned in the introduction to this book, the old paradigm has had negative consequences for our thinking about this important national issue and for our interventions, as well. In Chap. 1, I argued that one consequence of the "old paradigm" is that it has produced distortions that have harmed the relationship between law enforcement and the diverse communities that they serve. If some communities—such as racial and ethnic minorities—believe that biased policing is produced only by ill-intentioned police with explicit biases, and if they also believe that biased policing is widespread, they may come to believe that many or most police are ill-intentioned individuals. This apparently was the case for an African American community stakeholder who participated in a command-community Fair and Impartial Policing session held in California. After I finished presenting the science, he said, "I came in here thinking all cops were racist, and now I don't." He had entered the training room with a view reflecting the "old paradigm"; for him, biased policing was real and big; prior to the exposure to the science he had but one explanation: *all those ill-intentioned racist cops*. After hearing the science, his views about police changed.

Another consequence of the old paradigm is police defensiveness around this issue and the resulting inaction. As an example, a chief of a mid-sized east coast agency called me up to his department in 2000 to speak to his command staff about

© The Author(s) 2017
L.A. Fridell, *Producing Bias-Free Policing*,
SpringerBriefs in Translational Criminology, DOI 10.1007/978-3-319-33175-1_4

what his agency could do to address racially biased policing and the perceptions of it. This occurred prior to my own exposure to the modern science of bias and so the science had no part in my presentation. At the end of my talk, a command-level leader's comments were to the effect: *We can't implement any of those recommendations or we'll be admitting we are racist.* First of all, the powerful message in his statement was that the agency should do nothing about biased policing even though it was the top issue facing policing at that time. And why did he say that? His statement reflects the old paradigm: *If only racist cops produce bias in policing and our department addresses biased policing, we will be conveying to all the world that we have racist cops.*

So the *new* paradigm—produced by acknowledging what the science tells us about the various ways that bias can manifest—holds out hope for a new era of change. With the new paradigm, community members can be concerned about biased policing without assuming most or all cops are bad. With the new paradigm, police can be less defensive about the issue and open to change efforts. And with the new paradigm come implications for those change efforts. The science guides us in terms of ways that *individuals* in policing can reduce and manage their biases and provides guidance in terms of what *agency leaders* need to do to promote fair and impartial policing.

Next Steps for Agency Leaders

So how does an agency leader who is committed to fair and impartial policing proceed? The first step is to conduct a diagnosis of the agency. As mentioned above, it is difficult to measure biased policing and so one alternative is to understand community perceptions of it. In San Francisco, in 2006 and 2007, Chief Fong implemented focus groups around the city to gauge the sentiments of residents within various areas of the city. She targeted for these events, the communities that, historically, had more strained, negative relationships with the police. Trained facilitators met with 12 to 15 residents who had been invited and, without police in the room,[1] asked general questions about the police-community relationship and then questions focused on potential police bias. The questions were:

- What do you like about the police? What don't you like?
- What do police do in your neighborhood that *increases* resident trust of and respect for them? What do they do that *decreases* resident trust and respect?
- What do residents do to help produce a trusting relationship? What do residents do that hurts police-community trust? What could residents and/or police do together to make the relationship stronger?

---

[1]The absence of police personnel was to ensure an environment that would encourage participants to speak frankly and openly. An exception was one focus group held with both law enforcement and community member participants.

- Do the San Francisco P.D. officers treat all people the same or do they treat some types of people differently than others? Probes: Who is treated differently and how are they treated differently? Why? What needs to be done and what are you willing to do to help?

Just holding these focus groups, was a trust-building activity and, in addition to that benefit, Chief Fong learned about what biased policing "looked like" to various community members and what efforts might be welcome and effective.

An additional aspect of agency "diagnoses" is to review the coverage above of the Comprehensive Program to Produce Fair and Impartial Policing. In Chap. 3, I covered these areas within a Comprehensive Program:

- The leadership message conveying a commitment to fair and impartial policing
- Meaningful policy
- Recruitment, hiring and promotion
- Training and education
- Supervision
- Accountability mechanisms
- Measurement
- Outreach
- Operations.

Virtually, every agency will have some areas within the elements that are strong and likely some areas where there are weaknesses. The diagnosis involves moving through each element to identify those strengths and weaknesses and producing a plan to remedy the latter.

This diagnosis might be conducted by relevant unit heads that are logically linked to specific elements (e.g., Commander of Training, Deputy Chief in charge of Administration, and thus in charge of recruitment, hiring and promotion) or the diagnosis, as well as the plan development and implementation might be the charge of a specially formed group. Prince William County Police Department (PWCPD), for instance, an early adopter of the FIP training and perspective, formed an internal "Fair and Impartial Policing Committee" in 2011. According to Captain Miller, the committee is comprised of the following members who are appointed by the Chief of Police (personal communication, 10 December 2014):

- A chairperson,
- One assistant chief,
- The academy director,
- The Internal Affairs Commander,
- The Personnel Bureau Commander, and
- The Special Investigations Bureau Commander.

This group is charged with helping the agency to maintain excellence in "protecting civil rights and maintaining public trust through fair, impartial, reasonable, and lawful enforcement of the law" (personal communication, 10 December 2014). The group identifies strengths and weaknesses and recommends any changes that will promote the agency's efforts. Additionally, the Chief can direct the committee to conduct an in-depth review of an action, policy, procedure, or operation that might be impeding the bias-free-policing objective.

Another option is to develop a board—advisory to the chief or sheriff—that is comprised of *both* police personnel and community stakeholders. The community members should be formal or informal leaders who (a) represent the diverse communities in the jurisdiction (as defined by race/ethnicity, socioeconomic status, immigration status, sexual orientation, and so forth), (b) are credible and respected members of their communities—known to hold the police to account, and (c) can engage in a constructive manner with the department on a sensitive topic. Adding police personnel facilitates buy-in as efforts to promote fair and impartial policing are implemented. Utilizing a board to implement fair and impartial policing initiatives has four advantages over having the agency executive implement the changes without one:[2]

- Credibility: Having a board will give credibility to the efforts that the chief or sheriff pledges to implement.
- Visibility: The press will be much more interested in the story if the executive is reporting progress with representatives from the NAACP, ACLU, La Raza, Dreamers, and the Human Rights Campaign by his/her side.
- Accountability: The concerned community members on the board, in particular, can decrease the likelihood of "implementation failure." They can hold the executive to account and complain (e.g., to the press) if efforts stagnate.
- Wisdom: The community members and law enforcement personnel bring knowledge and wisdom to bear on the implementation efforts.

Leaders in the State of Kansas—also an early adopter of the science-based perspective—recognized the importance of a dialogue and partnerships between police and community members.[3] State legislation supports the creation of community advisory boards to guide and facilitate efforts to implement jurisdiction-specific comprehensive approaches for producing bias-free policing. The Office of the Attorney General provides training to advisory board members on the science of bias and the Comprehensive Program. As part of this training, the Kansas Law Enforcement Training Center has partnered with the Kansas African American Affairs Commission to hold Fair and Impartial Policing Community Advisory Board Training Academies. On the first day of the two-day academies, community members are educated about law enforcement decision-making processes (e.g., use

---

[2]Such a board could have a mandate beyond producing bias-free policing. For instance, in Minneapolis, Chief Harteau has set up the Chief's Advisory Council with the following mandate: "The Chief's Advisory Council is a conduit to advise and inform the chief on police-community issues. Many of these issues relate to our diverse communities and how to better build relationships to improve safety and improve public trust" (MPD 2014, p. 7).

[3]Under the leadership of Ed Pavey the director of the Kansas Law Enforcement Training Center, a unit of the University of Kansas, police personnel around the state are receiving training in the science-based perspective.

of force), and an evening dinner session promotes open dialogue between law enforcement executives and community members on various police practices that are susceptible to community concern or misunderstanding. On the second day, both the community members and police officials learn about the modern science of bias and the elements of the Comprehensive Program to Produce Fair and Impartial Policing. They leave the training session with preliminary action plans. Indicating that community members, too, embrace the new paradigm, is the statement of Dr. Mildred Edwards, former executive director of the African-American Affairs Commission, "the adoption of the Fair and Impartial Policing training model is one of the best things that Kansas has done" (personal communication, 13 October 2014).

Next Steps for Researchers

Certainly more research is needed to further guide police professionals in their quest to promote bias-free policing in their agencies. In this section, I outline some of the high-priority research.

Implicit bias research focuses on particular groups that are stereotyped (e.g., groups based on race, body weight, gender) or can focus on particular stereotypes (e.g., lazy, smart). Relevant to the police world, we have examined the substantial body of research that links particular racial groups to aggression/threat; I also shared some research affirming a link between Muslim appearance and threat and gender (being male) and threat. Research exploring threat/aggression stereotypes should be expanded to explore other groups that are (or are not) linked to crime/aggression.[4] This research might examine whether threat-stereotypes are linked to groups based on age, dress, socioeconomic class, mental disability, legal documentation, body size, and so forth.

The stereotype of aggression/threat is not the only stereotype, however, that might impact individuals in the policing profession. Additional research might examine what groups are stereotypically linked to specific types of crime, such as drug use, human trafficking, identity theft, multiple-victim shooting sprees, domestic violence, and burglary, to name a few. Research might additionally examine stereotypes associated with other characteristics important to policing, such as lying. Of course, for purposes of enhancing police training with the results of these studies, it would be valuable if law enforcement professionals were the subjects in the laboratory studies. And, when possible, laboratory findings should be followed by and compared to field studies (see e.g., Fridell and Lim 2016).

---

[4]One example of this expanded focus, albeit related to jurors not police, is the research conducted by Funk and Todorov (2013) looking at the impact of defendant facial tattoos on jury determinations of guilt.

Correll and others have raised the possibility that the activation and application of biases on the part of police may vary by neighborhood context (see e.g., Correll et al. 2014, 2007b). And these laboratory researchers have raised the intriguing possibility that certain assignments—for instance, assignments to special crime units such as gang or street-crime units—might have "pro-biasing effects (see Correll et al. 2014; Sim et al. 2013). These are important questions to explore with research.

Research could also examine the effectiveness of various bias-reduction techniques on individuals within police departments. These could be examined in laboratory settings, but to enhance external reliability and thus generalizability, experiments or quasi-experiments in the field are desirable. As an example, some chiefs and sheriffs are directing their personnel to have a certain "volume" of positive contacts with community members during their work week. If a chief or sheriff were willing to randomly assign officers (or units of officers working geographic areas) to the high-positive-contact or normal-positive-contact conditions, a partner-researcher could assess, after a sufficient period of time, whether this positive contact impacted officers' attitudes toward various groups with whom they have had contact.

Chapter 2 of the book described how individuals can implement "controlled responses" when they recognize their biases, but also in that section, I articulated some of the factors that might reduce a person's ability to implement controlled responses. Right now the research is mixed on whether fatigue has a negative impact on controlled responses (see Govorun and Payne 2006; Ma et al. 2013; James et al. 2015). Since fatigue is well-known to the policing profession, further examination of this issue is warranted.

While this book highlighted the potential of human biases to impact the many and varied decisions/action of police, the community frustration and anger that has characterized the post-Ferguson era has been particularly focused on police use of force, especially deadly force. There is much potential for research to enhance our understanding of both (1) what bias-related factors might impact officers' decisions to use force, and (2) what interventions can reduce errors, especially errors linked to stereotypes. Regarding the first, recall that two lines of research produced diametrically opposed results when examining the impact of subject race on officer decisions to shoot. The Correll-and-colleagues line of studies predict that officers—because of the Black-crime implicit bias—will be *over*-vigilant with racial/ethnic minorities, especially Blacks. The James-and-colleague studies predict that officers —due to "counter bias"—will be *under*-vigilant with racial/ethnic minorities. First of all, it is important to have research confirm the James et al. claim that their laboratory unfolding scenes closely reflect real-life policing decisions. They use this claim to generalize their laboratory findings to the real world of policing. There is one key difference, however, between their lab set-up and the real world. For the officer subjects, unlike officers in the real world, there are no significant consequences to their being under-vigilant with Blacks. In the real world, that under-vigilance could produce serious bodily injury or even death. While the laboratory (or training setting) will never match the real world experience of being in a potentially violent encounter with a subject, the realistic nature of the unfolding scenario could be enhanced if the simulator "shot back" as some do. (As mentioned above, researchers testing officers in laboratory settings have found different results depending on whether the officer is in the shoot-back or not-shoot-back condition.) The credibility of the findings of James and colleagues would be strengthened if they were replicated in shoot-back conditions.

If the counter-bias findings hold up, then it will be important for future research to examine the circumstances and factors that produce in officer shooting decisions the implicit bias outcome, the counter bias outcome, or neither. Whether an incident produces overvigilance (e.g., caused by implicit bias), undervigilance (e.g., caused by counter-bias) or neither when an officer is interacting with a racial/ethnic minority may depend on many factors, such as individual officer characteristics, agency characteristics including the quality and frequency of use-of-force training, and the climate of the country or jurisdiction.

In the training section, I highlighted the theory and preliminary research that indicates that scenario-based training that includes counterstereotypes in ambiguous-threat situations will make demographics "non-diagnostic" for threat—leading the officer to focus on other clues, such as hands and behavior. This needs to be further tested and, if the effectiveness is affirmed, research needs to determine the frequency and dosage of the training that is required to produce and sustain the desired conditioning effect in officers.

It is also desirable to measure the impact on police professionals of the Fair and Impartial Policing training, which is based on the scientific principles set forth in this book. As indicated in the section in Chap. 3 on measurement, it is extremely challenging to measure biased policing in the field (and thus difficult to measure biased policing on the part of individual officers), but a controlled study could and should evaluate the impact of the training on attitudes, knowledge and skills.

Concluding Remarks

As this book goes to press, we are ending an almost two-year period during which community concerns about biased policing have been expressed—sometimes violently—on the streets of large and small jurisdictions. The events in Ferguson in August 2014 might be identified as a turning point for the discussion of police bias. The community anger about abusive and biased policing that was precipitated by the events in Ferguson has been fed by each and every subsequent event—in New York City, Cleveland, North Charleston, Baltimore and Chicago. On the one hand, maybe the year is just another "blip" of concern-and-reform that will abate like others before it in North American history. *Or maybe something else is on the horizon.* With each and every decade, the police profession has gotten better. Compared to decades past, law enforcement is doing better at hiring, training, tactics, accountability, and police–community partnerships. More than ever, there are police leaders who are committed to making their agencies and the profession as a whole the best it can be—leaders committed to constitutional, respectful, and fair and impartial policing. Maybe this is a new beginning and not a "blip" in history. In the hopes that this is the case, the purpose of this book is to assist in these efforts.

References

Ahmed, A. M. (2010). Muslim discrimination: Evidence from two lost-letter experiments. *Journal of Applied Social Psychology, 40*(4), 888–898.

Allport, G. W. (1954/1979). *The nature of prejudice*. Palo Alto, CA: Addison-Wesley Publishing.

American Civil Liberties Union Foundation. (2013). *The war on marijuana in black and white*. New York, NY: ACLU.

American Civil Liberties Union Foundation of Massachusetts. (2014). *Black, brown and targeted: A report on Boston Police Department street encounters from 2007–2014*. Boston, Massachusetts: ACLU Foundation of Massachusetts.

Ammar, N. H., Orloff, L. E., Dutton, M. A., & Aguilar-Hass, G. (2005). Calls to police and police response: A case study of Latina immigrant women in the USA. *International Journal of Police Science & Management, 7*(4), 230–244.

Ammar, N., Couture-Carron, A., Alvi, S., & San Antonio, J. (2014). Experiences of Muslim and Non-Muslim battered immigrant women with the police in the United States: A closer understanding of commonalities and differences. *Violence Against Women, 19*(12), 1449–1471.

Amnesty International. (2005). *Stonewalled: Police abuse and misconduct against lesbians, gay, bisexual and transgender people in the US*. New York: Amnesty International USA.

Amodio, D. M., Harmon-Jones, E., & Devine, P. G. (2003). Individual differences in the activation and control of affective race bias as assessed by startle eyeblink response and self-report. *Journal of Personality and Social Psychology, 84*(4), 738–753.

Amodio, D. M., Harmon-Jones, E., Devine, P. G., Curtin, J. J., Hartley, S. L., & Covert, A. E. (2004). Neural signals for the detection of unintentional race bias. *Psychological Science, 15*(2), 88–93.

Amodio, D. M., & Mendoza, S. A. (2010). Implicit intergroup bias: Cognitive, affective, and motivational underpinnings. In B. Gawronski & B. K. Payne (Eds.), *Handbook of implicit social cognition* (pp. 253–274). New York, NY: The Guilford Press.

Axelson, R. D., Solow, C. M., Ferguson, K. J., & Cohen, M. B. (2010). Assessing implicit gender bias in medical student performance evaluations. *Evaluation and the Health Professions, 33*(3), 365–385.

Banaji, M. R., & Greenwald, A. G. (1995). Implicit gender stereotyping in judgments of fame. *Journal of Personality and Social Psychology, 68*(2), 181–198.

Bartley, J. J. (2006). An update on autism: Science, gender, and the law. *Gender Medicine, 3*(2), 73–78.

Baseheart, J. R., & Cox, T. C. (1993). Effects of police use of profanity on a receiver's perceptions of credibility. *Journal of Police and Criminal Psychology, 9*(2), 9–19.

Baumeister, R. F., Bratslavsky, E., Finkenauer, C., & Vohs, K. D. (2001). Bad is stronger than good. *Review of General Psychology, 5*, 323–370.

Beattie, G., Cohen, D., & McGuire, L. (2013). An exploration of possible unconscious ethnic biases in higher education: The role of implicit attitudes on selection for university posts. *Semiotica, 197*, 171–201.

© The Author(s) 2017
L.A. Fridell, *Producing Bias-Free Policing*,
SpringerBriefs in Translational Criminology, DOI 10.1007/978-3-319-33175-1

Bellafone, G. (2013, April 5). Arrests by the fashion police. *New York Times*. Retrieved from http://www.nytimes.com/2013/04/07/nyregion/arrests-by-the-fashion-police.html?_r=0

Bendick, M., Jr., Jackson, C., & Romero, J. (1996). Employment discrimination against older workers: An experimental study of hiring practices. *Journal of Aging and Social Policy, 8*(4), 25–46.

Bennett, M. W. (2010). Unraveling the Gordian Knot of implicit bias in jury selection: The problems of judge-dominated voir dire, the failed promise of *Batson*, and proposed solutions. *Harvard Law & Policy Review, 4*(1), 149–171.

Bertrand, M., Chugh, D., & Mullainathan, S. (2005). Implicit discrimination. *The American Economic Review, 95*(2), 94–98.

Bertrand, M., & Mullainathan, S. (2004). Are Emily and Greg more employable than Lakisha and Jamal? A field experiment on labor market discrimination. *The American Economic Review, 94* (4), 991–1013.

Bessenoff, G. R., & Sherman, J. W. (2000). Automatic and controlled components of prejudice toward fat people: Evaluation versus stereotype activation. *Social Cognition, 18*(4), 329–353.

Birkbeck, C., & Gabaldon, L. G. (1998). The effect of citizens' status and behavior on Venezuelan police officers' decisions to use force. *Policing & Society: An International Journal of Research and Policy, 8*(3), 315–338.

Black, D., & Reiss, A, Jr. (1967). *Studies in crime and law enforcement in major metropolitan areas*. Washington, DC: Supt. of Docs, US Government Printing Office.

Blair, I. V. (2002). The malleability of automatic stereotypes and prejudice. *Personality and Social Psychology Review, 6*(3), 242–261.

Blair, I. V., & Banaji, M. R. (1996). Automatic and controlled processes in stereotype priming. *Journal of Personality and Social Psychology, 70*(6), 1142–1163.

Blair, I. V., Ma, J. E., & Lenton, A. P. (2001). Imagining stereotypes away: The moderation of implicit stereotypes through mental imagery. *Journal of Personality and Social Psychology, 5* (81), 828–841.

Bratton, W., & Knobler, P. (1998). *Turnaround: How America's top cop reversed the crime epidemic*. New York: Random House.

Brewer, M. (1979). In-group bias in the minimal intergroup situation: A cognitive-motivational analysis. *Psychological Bulletin, 86*(2), 307–324.

Brown, M. K. (1981). *Working the street: Police discretion and the dilemmas of reform*. New York: Russell Sage.

Brown, J. M., & Langan, P. A. (2001). *Policing and homicide, 1976-98: Justifiable homicide by police, police officers murdered by felons*. Washington, DC: US Department of Justice, Office of Justice Programs.

Brown, R., & Zagefka, H. (2005). Ingroup affiliations and prejudice. In J. F. Dovidio, P. Glick, & L. A. Rudman (Eds.), *On the nature of prejudice: Fifty years after Allport* (pp. 54–70). Malden, MA: Blackwell Publishing.

Burger, L. (2014). RISE Award nominee: 3 ways an Ohio PD gained their community's trust. *PoliceOne.com*. Retrieved from at http://www.policeone.com/chiefs-sheriffs/articles/7474149-RISE-Award-Nominee-3-ways-an-Ohio-PD-gained-their-communitys-trust/

Cacioppo, J. T., & Berntson, G. G. (1994). Relationship between attitudes and evaluative space: A critical review, with emphasis on the separability of positive and negative substrates. *Psychological Bulletin, 115*(3), 401–423.

Carbado, D. W., & Harris, C. I. (2011). Undocumented criminal procedure. *UCLA Law Review, 58*, 1543–1616.

Carlson, D. K. (2004). *Racial profiling seen as pervasive, unjust*. Gallup, Inc. Retrieved from http://www.gallup.com/poll/12406/racial-profiling-seen-pervasive-unjust.aspx

Carlsson, M., & Rooth, D. O. (2007). Evidence of ethnic discrimination in the Swedish labor market using experimental data. *Labour Economics, 14*(4), 716–729.

Center for Constitutional Rights. (2012). *Stop and frisk: The human impact*. New York, NY: CCR.

Chambliss, W. (1994). Policing the ghetto underclass: The politics of law and law enforcement. *Social Problems, 41*(2), 177–194.

Chown, N. (2010). 'Do you have any difficulties that I may not be aware of?' A study of autism awareness and understanding in the UK police service. *International Journal of Police Science & Management, 12*(2), 256–273.

Colvin, R. A. (2012). *Gay and lesbian cops: Diversity and effective policing.* Boulder, CO: Lynne Rienner Publishers.

Commission of Peace Officer Standards and Training. (n.d.). *Racial profiling: Issues and Impact.* [Video]. West Sacramento, CA: POST.

COPS Office/IACP Leadership Project. (2009, June). *Law enforcement recruitment toolkit.* Washington, D.C.: USDOJ Office of Community Oriented Policing Services.

Correll, J., Hudson, S. M., Guillermo, S., & Ma, D. S. (2014). The police officer's dilemma: A decade of research on racial bias in the decision to shoot. *Social & Personality Psychology Compass, 8*(5), 201–213.

Correll, J., & Keesee, T. (2009). Racial bias in the decision to shoot? *The Police Chief, 5,* 54–58.

Correll, J., Park, B., Judd, C. M., & Wittenbrink, B. (2007). The influence of stereotypes on decisions to shoot. *European Journal of Social Psychology, 37*(6), 1102–1117.

Correll, J., Park, B., Judd, C. M., & Wittenbrink, B. (2002). The police officer's dilemma: Using ethnicity to disambiguate potentially threatening individuals. *Journal of Personality and Social Psychology, 86*(6), 1314–1329.

Correll, J., Park, B., Judd, C. M., Wittenbrink, B., Sadler, M. S., & Keesee, T. (2007). Across the thin blue line: Police officers and racial bias in the decision to shoot. *Journal of Personality and Social Psychology, 92*(6), 1006–1023.

Correll, J., Urland, G. R., & Ito, T. A. (2006). Event-related potentials and the decision to shoot: The role of threat perception and cognitive control. *Journal of Experimental Social Psychology, 42*(1), 120–128.

Correll, J., Wittenbrink, B., Axt, J., Miyake, A., & Goyle, A. (2015). *When practice makes prudent: Training, task complexity, and control over racial bias in the decision to shoot.* Manuscript submitted for publication.

Correll, J., Wittenbrink, B., Park, B., Judd, C. M., & Goyle, A. (2011). Dangerous enough: Moderating racial bias with contextual threat cues. *Journal of Experimental Social Psychology., 47*(1), 184–189.

Cox, W. T. L., Devine, P. G., Plant, E. A., & Schwartz, L. L. (2014). Toward a comprehensive understanding of officers' shooting decisions: No simple answers to this complex problem. *Basic and Applied Social Psychology, 36,* 356–364.

Cullen, F. T., & Gilbert, K. E. (1982). *Reaffirming rehabilitation: Policy, practice, and prospects.* Cincinnati, OH: Anderson Publishers.

Dasgupta, N. (2004). Implicit ingroup favoritism, outgroup favoritism, and their behavioral manifestations. *Social Justice Research, 17*(2), 143–169.

Dasgupta, N., & Asgari, S. (2004). Seeing is believing: Exposure to counter-stereotypic women leaders and its effect on the malleability of automatic gender stereotyping. *Journal of Experimental Social psychology, 40*(5), 642–658.

Dasgupta, N., & Greenwald, A. G. (2001). On the malleability of automatic attitudes: Combating automatic prejudice with images of admired and disliked individuals. *Journal of Personality and Social Psychology, 81*(5), 800–814.

Dasgupta, N., & Rivera, L. M. (2008). When social context matters: The influence of long-term contact and short-term exposure to admired, outgroup members on implicit attitudes and behavioral intentions. *Social Cognition, 26*(1), 112–123.

Davies, G., & Fagan, J. (2012). Crime and enforcement in immigrant neighborhoods: Evidence from New York City. *The ANNALS of the American Academy of Political and Social Science, 641*(1), 99–124.

Deaux, K., & Emswiller, E. (1974). Explanations of successful performance on sex-linked tasks: What is skill for the male is luck for the female. *Journal of Personality and Social Psychology, 29*(1), 80–85.

Demby, G. (2012, June 15). Stop and frisk too harsh on gay Blacks and Latinos, advocates say. *Huffington Post.* Retrieved from http://www.huffingtonpost.com/2012/06/15/stop-and-frisk-gay-blacks-latinos-transgender-nypd_n_1599470.html

DeNavas-Walt, C., & Proctor, B. D. (2014). *Income and poverty in the United States: 2013.* Washington, D.C.: US Department of Commerce.

Devine, P. G. (1989). Stereotypes and prejudice: Their automatic and controlled components. *Journal of Personality and Social Psychology, 56*(1), 5–18.

Devine, P. G., Forscher, P. S., Austin, A. J., & Cox, W. T. L. (2012). Long-term reduction in implicit race bias: A prejudice habit-breaking intervention. *Journal of Experimental Social Psychology, 48*(6), 1267–1278.

Devine, P. G., Monteith, M., Zuwerink, J. R., & Elliot, A. J. (1991). Prejudice with and without compunction. *Journal of Personality and Social Psychology, 60*(6), 817–830.

Dewan, S., & Williams, T. (2015, December 30). More officers facing charges, but few see jail. *New York Times,* A14.

District of Columbia Police Complaints Board. (2013, 21 November). *MPD enforcement of the district's window tint law: Report and recommendations of the Police Complaints Board to Mayor Vincent C. Gray, the Council of the District of Columbia, and Chief of Police Cathy L. Lanier.* Unpublished report.

Douglas, J. (2011). The criminalization of poverty: Montreal's policy of ticketing homeless youth for municipal and transportation by-law infractions. *Appeal: Review of Current Law and Law Reform, 16,* 49–64.

Dovidio, J. F., Brigham, J. C., Johnson, B. T., & Gaertner, S. L. (1996). Stereotyping, prejudice, and discrimination: Another look. In C. N. Macrae, C. Stangor, & M. Hewstone (Eds.), *Stereotypes and stereotyping* (pp. 276–319). New York: Guilford Press.

Dovidio, J. F., & Gaertner, S. L. (1999). Reducing prejudice: Combating intergroup biases. *Current Directions in Psychological Science, 8*(4), 101–105.

Dovidio, J. F., & Gaertner, S. L. O. (2000). Aversive racism and selection decisions, 1989 and 1999. *Psychological Science, 11*(4), 315–319.

Dovidio, J. F., Kawakami, K., & Gaertner, S. L. (2000). Reducing contemporary prejudice: Combating explicit and implicit bias at the individual and intergroup level. In S. Oskamp (Ed.), *Reducing prejudice and discrimination* (pp. 13–163). Mahwah, NJ: Lawrence Erlbaum.

Dovidio, J. F., Kawakami, K., & Gaertner, S. L. (2002). Implicit and explicit prejudice and interracial interaction. *Journal of Personality and Social Psychology, 82*(1), 62–68.

Dovidio, J. F., Kawakami, K., Smoak, N., & Gaertner, S. L. (2009). The nature of contemporary racial prejudice. In R. E. Petty, R. H. Fazio, & P. Brinol (Eds.), *Attitudes: Insights from the new implicit measures* (pp. 165–192). New York, NY: Psychology Press.

Dragom, C. (2015). The Dispatch. *The Police Chief, 6,* 8.

Drake, B. (2014). *Ferguson highlights deep divisions between blacks and whites in America.* Pew Research Center. Retrieved from http://www.pewresearch.org/fact-tank/2014/11/26/ferguson-highlights-deep-divisions-between-blacks-and-whites-in-america/

Duncan, B. L. (1976). Differential perception and attribution of intergroup violence: Testing the lower limits of stereotyping of Blacks. *Journal of Personality and Social Psychology, 34*(4), 590–598.

Early, S. (2014, 28 November). Police violence is not inevitable: Four ways a California police chief connected cops with communities. *YES! Magazine.* Retrieved from http://www.yesmagazine.org/peace-justice/police-violence-is-not-inevitable-four-ways-a-california-police-chief-connected-cops-with-communities

Eberhardt, J. L., Purdie, V. J., Goff, P. A., & Davies, P. G. (2004). Seeing black: Race, crime and visual processing. *Journal of Personality and Social Psychology, 87*(6), 876–893.

Eith, C., & Durose, M. R. (2011). *Contacts between police and the public, 2008.* Washington, DC: US Department of Justice, Bureau of Justice Statistics.

Elias, P. (2015, 1 February). Northern California chief's new approach revitalizes force. *New York Times.* Retrieved from http://www.nytimes.com/aponline/2015/02/01/us/ap-us-police-chief-joins-protest-.html?_r=0

Elliott, I., Thomas, S. D. M., & Ogloff, J. R. P. (2011). Procedural justice in contacts with the police: Testing a relational model of authority in a mixed methods study. *Psychology, Public Policy and Law, 17*(4), 592–610.

Ellis, L. (1988). The victimful-victimless crime distinction, and seven universal demographic correlates of victimful criminal behavior. *Personality and Individual Differences, 9*(3), 525–548.

Engel, R. S., & Calnon, J. M. (2004). Examining the influence of drivers' characteristics during traffic stops with police: Results from a national survey. *Justice Quarterly, 21*(1), 49–90.

Engel, R. S., Calnon, J. M., & Bernard, T. J. (2002). Theory and racial profiling: Shortcomings and future directions in research. *Justice Quarterly, 19*(2), 249–273.

Epp, C.R., Maynard-Moody, S., & Haider-Markel, D.P. (2014). *Pulled Over: How police stops define race and citizenship.* Chicago, IL: University of Chicago press.

Fachner, G., & Carter, S. (2015). *Collaborative reform initiative: An assessment of deadly force in the Philadelphia Police Department.* Unpublished report. Submitted by the CNA Corporation to the USDOJ Office of Community Oriented Policing Services.

Farrell, A. (2015). Explaining leniency: Organizational predictors of the differential treatment of men and women in traffic stops. *Crime & Delinquency, 61*(4), 509–537.

Fiske, S. (2008, summer). Are we born racist? *Greater Good,* 14–17.

Fiske, S. T., & Krieger, L. H. (2013). *Policy implications of unexamined discrimination: Gender bias in employment as a case study.* Princeton, NJ: Princeton University Press.

Floyd et al v. The City of New York. (S.D.N.Y 2013). 08 Civ. 1034 SAS HBP.

Freiburger, T. L., Pierce, P., Singleton, W., & Weiskopf, C. (2015). An evaluation of students talking it over with police (STOP) in Milwaukee Schools. *The Police Chief, 1,* 16–17.

French, A. R., Franz, T. M., Phelan, L. L., & Blaine, B. E. (2013). Reducing Muslim/Arab stereotypes through evaluative conditioning. *The Journal of Social Psychology, 153*(1), 6–9.

Fridell, L. (2004). *By the numbers: A guide for analyzing race data from vehicle stops.* Washington, DC: The Police Executive Research Forum.

Fridell, L. (2005). *Understanding race data from vehicle stops: A stakeholder's guide.* Washington, DC: The Police Executive Research Forum.

Fridell, L. (2008). Racially biased policing: The law enforcement response to the implicit Black-crime association. In M. Lynch, E. B. Patterson, & K. K. Childs (Eds.), *Racial divide: Race, ethnicity and criminal justice* (pp. 39–59). Monsey, NY: Criminal Justice Press.

Fridell, L. A., & Lim, H. (2016). Assessing the racial aspects of police force using the implicit- and counter-bias perspectives. *Journal of Criminal Justice, 44,* 36–48.

Fridell, L., & Scott, M. (2005). Law enforcement agency responses to racially biased policing and the perceptions of its practice. In R. G. Dunham & G. P. Alpert (Eds.), *Critical issues in policing* (5th ed., pp. 403–421). Prospect Heights, IL: Waveland Press.

Fyfe, J. J. (1982). Blind justice: Police shootings in Memphis. *The Journal of Criminal Law and Criminology, 73*(2), 702–722.

Gaertner, S. L., & Dovidio, J. F. (2000). *Reducing intergroup bias: The common ingroup identity model.* Philadelphia, PA: The Psychology Press.

Galinsky, A. D., & Moskowitz, G. B. (2000). Perspective-taking: Decreasing stereotype expression, stereotype accessibility, and in-group favoritism. *Journal of Personality & Social Psychology, 78*(4), 708–724.

Gelman, A., Fagan, J., & Kiss, A. (2007). An analysis of the New York City Police Department's "stop-and-frisk" policy in the context of claims of racial bias". *Journal of the American Statistical Association, 102*(479), 813–823.

Gilbert, D., & Hixon, J. G. (1991). The trouble of thinking: Activation and application of stereotypic beliefs. *Journal of Personality and Social Psychology, 60*(4), 509–517.

Gladwell, M. (2005). *Blink: The power of thinking without thinking.* New York, NY: Little, Brown and Company.

Goff, P. A., Eberhardt, J. L., Williams, M. J., & Jackson, M. C. (2008). Not yet human: Implicit knowledge, historical dehumanization, and contemporary consequences. *Journal of Personality and Social Psychology, 94*(2), 292–306.

Gonzales, C., Kim, M. Y., & Marantz, P. R. (2014). Implicit bias and its relation to health disparities: A teaching program and survey of medical students. *Teaching and Learning in Medicine, 26*(1), 64–71.

Govorun, O., & Payne, B. K. (2006). Ego-depletion and prejudice: Separating automatic and controlled components. *Social Cognition, 24*(2), 111–136.

Graham, S., & Lowery, B. S. (2004). Priming unconscious racial stereotypes about adolescent offenders. *Law and Human Behavior, 28*(5), 483–504.

Greenwald, A. G., & Krieger, L. H. (2006). Implicit bias: Scientific foundations. *California Law Review, 94*(4), 945–967.

Greenwald, A. G., McGhee, D. E., & Schwartz, J. L. K. (1998). Measuring individual differences in implicit cognition: The implicit association test. *Journal of Personality and Social Psychology, 74*(6), 1464–1480.

Greenwald, A. G., Oakes, M. A., & Hoffman, H. (2003). Targets of discrimination: Effects of race on responses to weapons holders. *Journal of Experimental Social Psychology, 39*, 399–405.

Gross, E. F., & Hardin, C. D. (2007). Implicit and explicit stereotyping of adolescents. *Social Justice Research, 20*(2), 140–160.

Haddad, A., Giglio, K., Keller, K. M., & Lim, N. (2012). *Increasing organizational diversity in 21st century policing: Lessons from the US Military.* Santa Monica, CA: Rand Corporation.

Hall, N. R., Crisp, R. J., & Suen, M. (2009). Reducing implicit prejudice by blurring intergroup boundaries. *Basic and Applied Social Psychology, 31*(3), 244–254.

Hardin, C. D., & Banaji, M. R. (2013). The nature of implicit prejudice: Implications for personal and public policy. In E. Shafir (Ed.), *The behavioral foundations of public policy* (pp. 13–31). Princeton, NJ: Princeton University Press.

Harris, L. T., & Fiske, S. T. (2011). Dehumanized perception: A psychological means to facilitate atrocities, torture, and genocide? *Journal of Psychology, 219*, 175–181.

Hebl, M. R., Foster, J. B., Mannix, L. M., & Dovidio, J. F. (2013). Formal and interpersonal discrimination: A field study of bias toward homosexual applicants. *Personality and Social Psychology Bulletin, 28*(6), 815–825.

Hernandez, R. A., Haidet, P., Gill, A. C., & Teal, C. R. (2013). Fostering students' reflection about bias in healthcare: Cognitive dissonance and the role of personal and normative standards. *Medical Teacher, 35*(4), e1082–e1089.

Hertel, G., & Kerr, N. L. (2001). Priming in-group favoritism: The impact of normative scripts in the minimal group paradigm. *Journal of Experimental Social Psychology, 37*(4), 316–324.

Higgins, G. E., Jennings, W. G., Jordan, K. L., & Gabbidon, S. L. (2011). Racial profiling in decisions to search: A preliminary analysis using propensity-score matching. *International Journal of Police Science and Management, 13*(4), 336–347.

Higgins, G. E., Vito, G. F., & Walsh, W. F. (2008). Searches: An understudied area of racial profiling. *Journal of Ethnicity in Criminal Justice, 6*(1), 23–39.

Hilton, J. L., & von Hippel, W. (1996). Stereotypes. *Annual Review of Psychology, 47*, 237–271.

Hipp, J. R. (2011). Spreading the wealth: The effect of the distribution of income and race/ethnicity across households and neighborhoods on city crime trajectories. *Criminology, 49*(3), 631–665.

Hoffmaster, D. A., Murphy, G., McFadden, S., & Griswold, M. (2010). *Police and immigration: How chiefs are leading their communities through the challenges.* Washington, DC: Police Executive Research Forum.

Independent Police Auditor, Bay Area Rapid Transit PD. (2014, February 10). *Policy recommendation—BPD Policy 401*. Memorandum. Available from the author.

International Association of Chiefs of Police. (2006). *Enforcing immigration law: The role of state, tribal and local law enforcement*. Arlington, VA: IACP.

International Association of Chiefs of Police. (2007). *A symbol of fairness and neutrality: Policing diverse communities in the 21st century*. Arlington, VA: IACP.

International Association of Chiefs of Police. (2015). *National policy summit on community-police relations: Advancing a culture of community cohesion and trust*. Alexandria, VA: IACP.

Jacobs, D., & O'Brien, R. (1998). The determinants of deadly force: A structural analysis of police violence. *The American journal of Sociology, 103*(4), 837–862.

James, L., Fridell, L., & Straub, F. (2016). Psychosocial factors impacting on officers' decisions to use deadly force: The Implicit Bias v. "Ferguson" Effects. *The Police Chief*, February, 44–51.

James, L., James, S., & Vila, B. (2015). *Does fatigue override police officers' fear of the consequences of shooting African American suspects? Insight into the relationship between fatigue, implicit racial bias, and decisions to shoot*. Manuscript under review: Washington State University at Spokane.

James, L., Klinger, D., & Vila, B. (2014). Racial and ethnic bias in decisions to shoot seen through a stronger lens: Experimental results from high-fidelity laboratory simulations. *Journal of Experimental Criminology, 10*(3), 323–340.

James, L., Vila, B., & Daratha, K. (2013). Influence of suspect race and ethnicity on decisions to shoot in high fidelity deadly force judgement and decision-making simulations. *Journal of Experimental Criminology, 9*(2), 189–212.

James, L., Vila, B., & James, S. (2016). The reverse racism effect: Are cops more hesitant to shoot black than white suspects? *Criminology and Public Policy, 6*.

Jones, J. M. (2015). *In U.S., confidence in the police lowest in 22 years*. Gallup, Inc. Retrieved from http://www.gallup.com/poll/183704/confidence-police-lowest-years.aspx

Jost, J. T., Rudman, L. A., Blair, I. V., Carney, D. R., Dasgupta, N., Glaser, J., & Hardin, C. D. (2009). The existence of implicit bias is beyond reasonable doubt: A refutation of ideological and methodological objections and executive summary of ten studies that no manager should ignore. *Research in Organizational Behavior, 29*, 39–69.

Kang, J., Bennett, M., Carbado, D., Casey, P., Dasgupta, N., Faigman, D., et al. (2012). Implicit bias in the courtroom. *UCLA Law Review, 59*(5), 1124–1186.

Kang, J., & Lane, K. (2010). Seeing through colorblindness: Implicit bias and the law. *UCLA Law Review, 58*(2), 465–520.

Karpinski, A., & Hilton, J. L. (2001). Attitudes and the implicit association test. *Journal of Personality and Social Psychology, 81*(5), 774–788.

Kasdan, A. (2006). Increasing diversity in police departments: Strategies and tools for human rights commissions and others. *Executive Session Papers: Human Rights Commissions and Criminal Justice*. Retrieved from http://www.hks.harvard.edu/content/download/67469/1242686/version/1/file/increasing_police_diversity.pdf

Kawakami, K., Dovidio, J. F., Moll, J., Hermsen, S., & Russin, A. (2000). Just say no (to stereotyping), Effects of training in the negation of stereotypic associations on stereotype activation. *Journal of Personality and Social Psychology, 78*(5), 871–888.

Kelling, G. (2015, August 11). Don't blame my 'broken windows' theory for poor policing. *Politico*. Retrieved from http://www.politico.com/magazine/story/2015/08/broken-windows-theory-poor-policing-ferguson-kelling-121268

Kewley, G. (2002). ADHD and youth justice. In C. Dale & L. Storey (Eds.), *Care and treatment of offenders with learning disabilities*. Paper presented at the International Conference on the Care and Treatment of Offenders with a Learning Disability, University of Central Lancashire, Preston, 4–6 September 2001. Retrieved from http://www.ldoffenders.co.uk/conferences/1stCon2001/1stConDocuments/01partFIVEsn.doc

Khashu, A. (2009). *The role of local police: Striking a balance between immigration enforcement and civil liberties*. Washington, DC: Police Foundation.

Klinger, D. (2004). *Into the kill zone: A cop's eye view of deadly force.* San Francisco, CA: Jossey-Bass.

Kochel, T. R., Wilson, D. B., & Mastrofski, S. D. (2011). Effect of suspect race on officers' arrest decisions. *Criminology, 49*(2), 473–512.

Krivo, L. J., & Peterson, R. D. (1996). Extremely disadvantaged neighborhoods and urban crime. *Social Forces, 75*(2), 619–648.

Kubrin, C. E., & Weitzer, R. (2003). Retaliatory homicide: Concentrated disadvantage and neighborhood culture. *Social Problems, 50*(2), 157–180.

LaVigne, N. G., Lachman, P., Rao, S., & Matthews, A. (2014). *Stop and frisk: Balancing crime control with community relations.* Washington, DC: Office of Community Oriented Policing Services.

Lambert, A., Payne, B., Jacoby, L., Shaffer, L., Chasteen, A., & Khan, S. (2003). Stereotypes as dominant responses: On the "social facilitation" of prejudice in anticipated public contexts. *Journal of Personality & Social Psychology, 84*(2), 277–295.

Langton, L., & Durose, M. (2013). *Police behavior during traffic and street stops, 2011.* Washington, DC: US Department of Justice, Bureau of Justice Statistics.

Lee, J., & Gibbs, J. (2015). Race and attitudes toward the police: The mediating effect of social distance. *Policing: An International Journal of Police Strategies and management, 38*(2), 314–332.

Leiber, M. J. (2008). Theories of racial and ethnic bias. In M. Lynch, E. B. Patterson, & K. Childs (Eds.), *Racial divide: Race, ethnicity and criminal justice theories of racial and ethnic bias* (pp. 15–38). Monsey, NY: Criminal Justice Press.

Levinson, J. D., & Young, D. (2010). Different shades of bias: Skin tone, implicit racial bias and judgments of ambiguous evidence. *West Virginia Law Review, 112*, 307–350.

Levy, B. (1996). Improving memory in old age through implicit self-stereotyping. *Journal of Personality and Social Psychology, 71*(6), 1092–1107.

Liederbach, J. (2007). Controlling suburban and small-town hoods: An examination of police encounters with juveniles. *Youth Violence and Juvenile Justice, 5*(2), 107–124.

Lin, A. C., & Harris, D. R. (2009). *The colors of poverty: Why racial & ethnic disparities persist.* Ann Arbor, MI: National Poverty Center.

Lublin, J. S. (2014, January 9). Bringing hidden biases into the light: Big businesses teach staffers how 'unconscious bias' impacts on decisions. *Wall Street Journal.* Retrieved from http://www.wsj.com/articles/SB10001424052702303754404579308562690896896

Lum, C., & Nagin, D. (2015). Reinventing American policing: A seven-point blueprint for the 21st century. *Translational Criminology, Fall,* 2–5, 11.

Lundman, R. J., & Kaufman, R. L. (2003). Driving while black: Effects of race, ethnicity, and gender on citizen self-reports of traffic stops and police actions. *Criminology, 41*(1), 195–220.

Lybarger, J. E., & Monteith, M. J. (2011). The effect of Obama saliency on individual level racial bias: Silver bullet or smokescreen? *Journal of Experimental Social Psychology, 47*(3), 647–652.

Ma, D. S., Correll, J., Wittenbrink, B., Bar-Anan, Y., Sriram, N., & Nosek, B. (2013). When fatigue turns deadly: The association between fatigue and racial bias in the decision to shoot. *Basic and Applied Social Psychology, 35*(6), 515–524.

Macartney, S., Bishaw, A., & Fontenot, K. (2013). *Poverty rates for selected detailed race and Hispanic groups by state and place: 2007–2011.* Washington, D. C.: US Department of Commerce.

MacDonald, J. M. (2001). Analytic methods for examining race and ethnic disparity in the juvenile courts. *Journal of Criminal Justice, 29*(6), 187–205.

MacDonald, J. M. (2003). The effect of ethnicity on juvenile court decision making in Hawaii. *Youth & Society, 35*(2), 243–263.

Macrae, C. N., Bodenhausen, G. V., & Milne, A. B. (1998). Saying no to unwanted thoughts: Self-focus and the regulation of mental life. *Journal of Personality and Social Psychology, 74*(3), 578–590.

Macrae, C. N., Milne, A. B., & Bodenhausen, G. V. (1994). Stereotype as energy-saving devices: A peek inside the cognitive toolbox. *Journal of Personality and Social Psychology, 66*, 37–47.

Magnus, C. (2015, May 20). Guest commentary: Richmond police get extensive training in appropriate use of force. *Contra Costa Times*. Retrieved from http://www.contracostatimes.com/opinion/ci_28119426/guest-commentary-richmond-police-get-extensive-training-appropriate

Major City Chiefs Police Association. (2011, October). *Revised immigration position*. Major City Chiefs Police Association Position Paper. Retrieved from https://www.majorcitieschiefs.com/pdf/news/immigration_position102311.pdf

Mather, K. (2015, December 15). LAPD found no bias in all 1356 complaints. *Los Angeles Times*, December 15. Retrieved from http://www.latimes.com/local/lanow/la-me-ln-lapd-biased-policing-report-20151215-story.html

Matthies, C. F., Keller, K. M., & Lim, N. (2012). *Identifying barriers to diversity in law enforcement*. Santa Monica, CA: RAND Corporation.

Mazerolle, L., Antrobus, E., Bennett, S., & Tyler, T. R. (2013). Shaping citizen perceptions of police legitimacy: A randomized field trial of procedural justice. *Criminology, 51*(1), 33–63.

McConnell, A. R., & Liebold, J. M. (2001). Relations among the implicit association test, discriminatory behavior, and explicit measures of attitudes. *Journal of Experimental Social Psychology, 37*(5), 435–442.

McNulty, T. L., & Bellair, P. E. (2003). Explaining racial and ethnic differences in adolescent violence: Structural disadvantage, family well-being, and social capital. *Justice Quarterly, 20* (1), 1–31.

Meehan, A. J., & Ponder, M. C. (2002). Race and place: The ecology of racial profiling African American motorists. *Justice Quarterly, 19*(3), 399–430.

Minneapolis Police Department. (2014). *Moving the dial in the Minneapolis Police Department*. Unpublished document. Minneapolis, MN: Minneapolis PD.

Mitchell, O., & Caudy, M. S. (2015). Examining racial disparities in drug arrests. *Justice Quarterly, 32*(2), 288–313.

Mitchell, T. L., Haw, R. M., Pfeifer, J. E., & Meissner, C. A. (2005). Racial bias in mock juror decision-making: A meta-analytic review of defendant treatment. *Law and Human Behavior, 29*(6), 621–637.

Monteith, M. J. (1993). Self-regulation of prejudiced responses: Implications for progress in prejudice-reduction efforts. *Journal of Personality and Social Psychology, 65*(3), 469–485.

Monteith, M. J. (1996). Affective reactions to prejudice-related discrepant responses: The impact of standard salience. *Personality and Social Psychology Bulletin, 22*(1), 48–59.

Monteith, M. J., Arthur, S. A., & Flynn, S. M. (2010). Self-regulation and bias. In J. F. Dovidio, M. Hewstone, P. Glick, & V. M. Esses (Eds.), *The SAGE handbook of prejudice, stereotyping and discrimination* (pp. 493–507). Los Angeles, CA: Sage Publications.

Monteith, M. J., Ashburn-Nardo, L., Voils, C. I., & Czopp, A. M. (2002). Putting the brakes on prejudice: On the development and operation of cues for control. *Journal of Personality and Social Psychology, 83*(5), 1029–1050.

Monteith, M. J., Devine, P. G., & Zuwerink, J. R. (1993). Self-directed vs. other-directed affect as a consequence of prejudice-related discrepancies. *Journal of Personality and Social Psychology, 64*(2), 198–210.

Monteith, M. J., Sherman, J. W., & Devine, P. G. (1998). Suppression as a stereotype control strategy. *Personality and Social Psychology Review, 2*(1), 63–82.

Morrison, G. B., & Garner, T. K. (2011). Latitude in deadly force training: Progress or problem? *Police Practice and Research, 12*(4), 341–361.

Murphy, B. (2015, January 9). A model for police reform. *The Richmond Pulse, 33*.

NAACP. (2014). *Born Suspect: Stop-and-frisk abuses and the continued fight to end racial profiling in America*. Baltimore, MD: National Association for the Advancement of Colored People.

National Center for State Courts. (n.d.). *Helping courts address implicit bias: Resources for education*. Retrieved from http://www.ncsc.org/ibeducation

National Highway Traffic Safety Administration. (2014). *Data-driven approaches to crime and traffic safety (DDACTS): Operational guidelines*. Washington, DC: United States Department of Transportation.

New York State Task Force on Police-on-Police Shootings. (2010). *Reducing inherent danger: Report of the task force on police-on-police shootings*. Retrieved from http://www.hks.harvard.edu/criminaljustice-backup/publications/Police-on-Police_Shootings.pdf

Norton, M. I., Vandello, J. A., & Darley, J. M. (2004). Casuistry and social category bias. *Journal of Personality and Social Psychology, 87*(6), 817–831.

Nosek, B. A., Banaji, M. R., & Greenwald, A. G. (2002). Harvesting implicit group attitudes and beliefs from a demonstration website. *Group Dynamics, 6*(1), 101–115.

Obbie, M. (2015, September 3). This is a fundamentally different way of policing. *Slate*. Retrieved from http://www.slate.com/articles/news_and_politics/crime/2015/09/meet_susan_herman_the_woman_bill_bratton_has_tasked_with_repairing_the_nypd.single.html

Oberle, C. D., Nagurney, A. J., & Lee, C. N. (2011). Implicit prejudicial biases in student learning: The effects of sexual orientation. *Journal of Homosexuality, 58*(4), 447–461.

Office of Community Oriented Policing Services. (2013). Coffee with a cop: Building trust with the community one cup at a time. *Dispatch, 6*(12). Retrieved from http://cops.usdoj.gov/html/dispatch/12-2013/coffe_with_a_cop.asp

Oliver, P. (2014). *Recruitment, selection and retention of law enforcement*. Flushing, NY: Looseleaf Law Publications.

Ontario Association of Chiefs of Police. (2013). *Best practices in policing and LGBTQ communities in Ontario*. Toronto: OACP Diversity Committee.

Opotow, S. (1990). Moral exclusion and injustice: An introduction. *Journal of Social Issues, 46*, 1–20.

Ousey, G. C. (1999). Homicide, structural factors, and the racial invariance assumption. *Criminology, 37*(2), 405–426.

Paluck, E. L. (2012). Interventions aimed at the reduction of prejudice and conflict. In L. Tropp (Ed.), *Oxford Handbook of Intergroup Conflict* (pp. 179–192). Oxford: Oxford University Press.

Paluck, E. L., & Green, D. P. (2009). Prejudice reduction: What works? A review and assessment of research and practice. *Annual Review of Psychology, 60*, 339–367.

Parascandola, R., Tracy, T., & McShane, L. (2015, March 26). NYPD Commissioner Bratton predicts cops will have 1 million fewer law enforcement contacts with public in 2015. *New York Daily News*. Retrieved from http://www.nydailynews.com/new-york/nyc-crime/exclusive-bratton-predicts-nypd-public-contacts-fall-1m-article-1.2162742

Park, J., Felix, K., & Lee, G. (2007). Implicit attitudes toward Arab-Muslims and the moderating effects of social information. *Basic and Applied Social Psychology, 29*(1), 35–45.

Park, J., Malachi, E., Sternin, O., & Tevet, R. (2009). Subtle bias against Muslim job applicants in personnel decisions. *Journal of Applied Social Psychology, 39*(9), 2174–2190.

Payne, B. K. (2001). Prejudice and perception: The role of automatic and controlled processes in misperceiving a weapon. *Journal of Personality and Social Psychology, 81*(2), 181–192.

Payne, B. K. (2006). Weapon Bias: Split-second decisions and unintended stereotyping. *Current Directions in Psychological Science, 15*(6), 287–291.

Payne, B. K., Lambert, A. J., & Jacoby, L. L. (2002). Best laid plans: Effects of goals on accessibility bias and cognitive control in race-based misperceptions of weapons. *Journal of Experimental Social Psychology, 38*(4), 384–396.

Perdue, C. W., Dovidio, J. F., Gurtman, M. B., & Tyler, R. B. (1990). Us and them: Social categorization and the process of intergroup bias. *Journal of Personality and Social Psychology, 59*(3), 475–486.

Peruche, B. M., & Plant, E. A. (2005). The consequences of race for police officers' responses to criminal suspects. *Psychological Science, 16*(3), 180–183.

Peruche, B. M., & Plant, E. A. (2006). The correlates of law enforcement officers' automatic and controlled race-based responses to criminal suspects. *Basic and Applied Social Psychology, 28* (2), 193–199.

Pettigrew, T. F., & Tropp, L. R. (2006). A meta-analytic test of intergroup contact theory. *Journal of Personality and Social Psychology, 90*(5), 751–783.

Petty, R. E., Fazio, R. H., & Brinol, P. (2009). The new implicit measures: An overview. In R. E. Petty, R. H. Fazio, & P. Brinol (Eds.), *Attitudes: Insights from the new implicit measures* (pp. 3–18). New York, NY: Psychology Press.

Pisarski, A. (Ed.). (1994). *Nobody listens: The experience of contact between young people and police.* Sydney: Youth Justice Coalition of NSW.

Plant, A. E., & Devine, P. G. (1998). Internal and external motivation to respond without prejudice. *Journal of Personality and Social Psychology, 75*(3), 811–832.

Plant, E. A., & Peruche, B. M. (2005). The consequences of race for police officers' responses to criminal suspects. *Psychological Science, 16*(3), 180–183.

Plant, A. E., Peruche, M. B., & Butz, D. A. (2005). Eliminating automatic racial bias: Making race non-diagnostic for responses to criminal suspects. *Journal of Experimental Social Psychology, 41*(2), 141–156.

Police Executive Research Forum. (2012). *Voices from across the country: Local law enforcement officials discuss the challenges of immigration enforcement.* Washington, DC: PERF.

Police Executive Research Forum. (2014a). *Legitimacy and procedural justice: A new element of police leadership.* Washington, D.C.: PERF.

Police Executive Research Forum. (2014b). *Legitimacy and procedural justice: The New Orleans case study.* Washington, D.C.: PERF.

Police Executive Research Forum. (2015). *Re-engineering training on police use of force.* Washington, DC: PERF.

Pratt, T. C., & Cullen, F. T. (2005). Assessing macro-level predictors and theories of crime: A meta-analysis. *Crime and Justice, 32*, 373–450.

President's Task Force on 21st Century Policing. (2015). *Final report of the president's task force on twenty-first century policing.* Washington, DC: Office of Community Oriented Policing Services.

Proctor, J., Clemmons, A., & Rosenthal, R. (2009). Discourteous cops and unruly citizens: Improving police-citizen satisfaction through mediation. *Community Policing Dispatch, 2*(3).

Pronin, E., Lin, D. Y., & Ross, L. (2002). The bias blind spot: Perceptions of bias in self versus others. *Personality and Social Psychology Bulletin, 28*(3), 369–381.

Pronin, E., & Schmidt, K. (2013). Claims and denials of bias and their implications for policy. In E. Shafir (Ed.), *The behavioral foundations of public policy* (pp. 196–216). Princeton, NJ: Princeton University Press.

Rachlinski, J. J., Johnson, S. L., Wistrich, A. J., & Guthrie, C. (2009). Does unconscious racial bias affect trial judges? *Notre Dame Law Review, 84*(3), 1195–1246.

Rahr, S., & Rice, S. K. (2015). *From warriors to guardians: Recommitting American police culture to democratic ideals.* New Perspectives in Policing Bulletin, NCJ 248654. Washington, D.C.: US Department of Justice, National Institute of Justice.

Reskin, B. (2005). Unconsciousness raising. *Regional Review, 14*(3), 32–37.

Riach, P. A., & Rich, J. (2002). Field experiments of discrimination in the market place. *The Economic Journal, 112*(483), F480–F518.

Richardson, L. S., & Goff, P. A. (2013). Implicit racial bias in public defender triage. *The Yale Law Journal, 122*(8), 2626–2649.

Ridgeway, G., Mitchell, O., Gunderman, S., Alexander, C., & Letten, J. (2016). *An examination of racial disparities in bicycle stops and citations made by the Tampa Police Department.* Washington, DC: Office of Community Oriented Police Services.

Rogers, R., & DeBolt, D. (2014, September 6). Use of deadly force by police disappears on Richmond streets. *Contra Costa Times.* Retrieved from http://www.contracostatimes.com/news/ci_26482775/use-deadly-force-by-police-disappears-richmond-streets

Romney, L. (2015, May 6). Homicide rates drop as Richmond chief builds bond with community. *Los Angeles Times*. Retrieved from http://www.latimes.com/local/crime/la-me-richmond-pd-20150503-story.html

Rooth, D. O. (2007). *Implicit discrimination in Hiring: Real world evidence*. Bonn, Germany: Institute for the Study of Labor.

Rosenfeld, R., Rojek, J., & Decker, S. (2011). Age matters: Race differences in police searches of young and older male drivers. *Journal of Research in Crime and Delinquency, 49*(1), 31–55.

Ross, H. J. (2014). *Everyday bias: Identifying and navigating unconscious judgments in our daily lives*. Lanham, MD: Rowman & Littlefield.

Rudman, L. A. (2004). Social justice in our minds, homes and society: The nature, causes, and consequences of implicit bias. *Social Justice Research, 17*(2), 129–142.

Rudman, L. A., Ashmore, R. D., & Gary, M. L. (2001). `Unlearning' automatic biases: The malleability of implicit prejudice and stereotypes. *Journal of Personality and Social Psychology, 81*(5), 856–868.

Sadler, M. S., Correll, J., Park, B., & Judd, C. M. (2012). The world is not black and white: Racial bias in the decision to shoot in a multiethnic context. *Journal of Social Issues, 68*(2), 286–313.

Saint-Fort, P., Yasso, N., & Shah, S. (2012). *Engaging police in immigrant communities: Promising practices from the field*. New York: Vera Institute of Justice.

Sampson, R. J., & Lauritsen, J. L. (1997). Racial and ethnic disparities in crime and criminal justice in the United States. *Crime and Justice, 21*, 311–374.

Sampson, R. J., Morenoff, J. D., & Raudenbush, S. (2005). Social anatomy of racial and ethnic disparities in violence. *American Journal of Public Health, 95*(2), 224–232.

Schmidt, K., & Nosek, B. A. (2010). Implicit (and explicit) race attitudes barely changed during Barack Obama's presidential campaign and early presidency. *Journal of Experimental Social Psychology, 46*(2), 308–314.

Schofield, T. P., Deckman, T., Garris, C. P., DeWall, C. N., & Denson, T. F. (2015). Brief report: Evidence of ingroup bias on the shooter task in a Saudi sample. *Sage Open,*. doi:10.1177/2158244015576057.

Schulman, K. A., Berlin, J. A., Harless, W., Kerner, J. F., Sistrunk, S., Gersh, B. J., et al. (1999). The effect of race and sex on physicians' recommendations for cardiac catheterization. *The New England Journal of Medicine, 340*(8), 618–626.

Schuman, H., Steeh, C., Bobo, L., & Krysan, M. (1997). *Racial attitudes in America: Trends and Interpretations* (Revised ed.). Cambridge, MA: Harvard University Press.

Schwartz, M. B., Vartanian, L. R., Nosek, B. A., & Brownell, K. D. (2006). The influence of one's own body weight on implicit and explicit anti-fat bias. *Obesity, 14*(3), 440–447.

Sherman, L. W., Gartin, P. R., & Buerger, M. E. (1989). Hot spots of predatory crime: Routine activities and the criminology of place. *Criminology, 27*(1), 27–56.

Shih, M. J., Stotzer, R., & Gutierrez, A. S. (2013). Perspective-taking and empathy: Generalizing the reduction of group bias towards Asian Americans to general outgroups. *Journal of Abnormal Psychology, 4*(2), 79–83.

Sim, J. J., Correll, J., & Sadler, M. S. (2013). Understanding police and expert performance: When training attenuates (vs. exacerbates) stereotypic bias in the decision to shoot. *Personality and Social Psychology Bulletin, 39*(3), 291–304.

Smith, D. A. (1986). The neighborhood context of police behavior. In. A. J. Reiss, Jr. & M. Tonry (Eds.), *Communities and crime* (pp. 313–341). Chicago: University of Chicago Press.

Smith, D. A., Visher, C. A., & Davidson, L. A. (1984). Equity and discretionary justice: The influence of race on police arrest decisions. *Journal of Criminal Law and Criminology, 75*(1), 234–249.

Smith, M. R., Makarios, M., & Alpert, G. P. (2006). Differential suspicion: Theory specification and gender effects in the traffic stop context. *Justice Quarterly, 23*(2), 271–295.

Smith, R. J., & Levinson, J. D. (2012). The impact of implicit racial bias on the exercise of prosecutorial discretion. *Seattle University Law Review, 35*, 795–826.

Sorenson, J., Marquart, J., & Brock, D. (1993). Factors relating to killings of felons by police officers: A test of the community violence and conflict hypotheses. *Justice Quarterly, 10*(3), 417–440.

Staats, C. (2013). *State of the science: Implicit bias review 2013*. Columbus, OH: Kirwan Institute for the Study of Race and Ethnicity.

Staats, C. (2014). *State of the science: Implicit bias review 2014*. Columbus, OH: Kirwan Institute for the Study of Race and Ethnicity.

Staats, C., Capatosto, K., Wright, R. A., & Contractor, D. (2015). *State of the science: Implicit bias review 2015*. Columbus, OH: Kirwan Institute for the Study of Race and Ethnicity.

Stone, J., & Moskowitz, G. B. (2011). Non-conscious bias in medical decision making: What can be done to reduce it? *Medical Education, 45*(8), 768–776.

Stoughton, S. I. A. C. P. (2015). Law enforcement's "warrior" problem. *Harvard Law Review Forum, 28*, 225–234.

StreetCred. (2015). *Unarmed civilians & the police: Analysis of the StreetCred police killings in context data*. Retrieved from http://www.streetcredsoftware.com/wp-content/uploads/2015/10/StreetCred_PKIC_Study_7_Oct_2015_1.02.pdf

Sunshine, J., & Tyler, T. R. (2003). The role of procedural justice and legitimacy in shaping public support for policing. *Law and Society Review, 37*(3), 513–548.

Swim, J. K., & Sanna, L. J. (1996). He's skilled, she's lucky: A meta-analysis of observers' attributions for women's and men's successes and failures. *Personality and Social Psychology Bulletin, 22*(5), 507–519.

Tajfel, H. (1982). Social psychology of intergroup relations. *Annual Review of Psychology, 33*, 1–39.

Tausch, N., & Hewstone, M. (2010). Intergroup contact. In J. F. Dovidio, M. Hewstone, P. Glick, & V. M. Esses (Eds.), *The SAGE handbook of prejudice, stereotyping and discrimination* (pp. 544–560). Los Angeles, CA: Sage Publications.

Teachman, B. A., Gapinski, K. D., Brownell, K. D., Rawlins, M., & Jeyaram, S. (2003). Demonstrations of implicit anti-fat bias: The impact of providing causal information and evoking empathy. *Health Psychology, 22*(1), 68–78.

Tenenbaum, H. R., & Ruck, M. D. (2007). Are teachers' expectations different for racial minority than for European American students? A meta-analysis. *Journal of Educational Psychology, 99*(2), 253–273.

Terrill, W., & Mastrofski, S. D. (2002). Situational and officer based determinants of police coercion. *Justice Quarterly, 19*(2), 215–248.

Terry v. Ohio. (1968). 302 U.S. 1.

Tomaskovic-Devey, D., Mason, M., & Zingraff, M. (2004). Looking for the driving while black phenomena: Conceptualizing racial bias processes and their associated distributions. *Police Quarterly, 7*(1), 3–29.

Toronto Police Service. (2013). *The police and community engagement review (The PACER report): Phase II—Internal report and recommendations*. Retrieved from http://www.torontopolice.on.ca/publications/files/reports/2013pacerreport.pdf

Tyler, T. R. (1990). *Why people obey the law*. New Haven, CT: Yale University Press.

Tyler, T. R. (2004). Enhancing police legitimacy. *The Annals of Political and Social Science,593*, 84–96.

Tyler, T. R., Goff, P. A., & MacCoun, R. J. (2015). The impact of psychological science on policing in the United States: Procedural justice, legitimacy, and effective law enforcement. *Psychological Science in the Public Interest, 16*(3), 75–109.

Uhlmann, E. L., & Cohen, G. L. (2005). Constructed criteria: Redefining merit to justify discrimination. *Psychological Science, 16*(6), 474–480.

United States Conference of Mayors. (2015). *Strengthening police-community relations in America's cities: A report of the US Conference of Mayors working group of mayors and police chiefs*. Washington, DC: US Conference of Mayors.

United States Department of Justice. (2014, December). *Guidance for federal law enforcement agencies regarding the use of race, ethnicity, gender, national origin, religion, sexual orientation or gender identity*. Washington, DC: US Department of Justice.

Unkelbach, C., Forgas, J. P., & Denson, T. F. (2008). The turban effect: The influence of Muslim headgear and induced affect on aggressive responses in the shooter bias paradigm. *Journal of Experimental Social Psychology, 44*(5), 1409–1413.

Van den Bergh, L., Denessen, E., Hornstra, L., Voeten, M., & Holland, R. W. (2010). The implicit prejudiced attitudes of teachers: Relations to teacher expectations and the ethnic achievement gap. *American Educational Research Journal, 47*(2), 497–527.

Van Ryn, M., & Saha, S. (2011). Exploring unconscious bias in disparities research and medical education. *Journal of the American Medical Association, 306*(9), 995–996.

Vescio, T. K., Sechrist, G. B., & Paolucci, M. P. (2003). Perspective taking and prejudice reduction: The mediational role of empathy arousal and situational attributions. *European Journal of Social Psychology, 33*(4), 455–472.

Vieraitis, L. M. (2000). Income inequality, poverty, and violent crime: A review of the empirical evidence. *Social Pathology, 6*(1), 24–45.

Walker, S. (2015, November). The war for the soul of American Policing. *SamuelWalker.net*. Retrieved from http://samuelwalker.net/wp-content/uploads/2015/12/WAR-FOR-THE-SOUL-Final.pdf

Walker, S., Spohn, C., & DeLone, M. (2000). *The color of justice* (2nd ed.). Belmont: Wadsworth Publishing.

Warren, P., Tomaskovic-Devey, D., Smith, W., Zingraff, M., & Mason, M. (2006). Driving while black: Bias processes and racial disparity in police stops. *Criminology, 44*(3), 709–738.

Wasserman, R., & Ginsburg, R. (2014). *Building relationships of trust: Moving to implementation*. Tallahassee, FL: Institute for Intergovernmental Research.

Weise, E. (2015, September 24). No deaths, no drama: A creed for Calif. police. *USA Today*, 14A.

Weisse, C. S., Sorum, P. C., Sanders, K. N., & Syat, B. L. (2001). Do gender and race affect decisions about pain management? *Journal of General Internal Medicine, 16*(4), 211–217.

West, M. H. (2001). *Community centered policing: A force for change*. New York, NY: PolicyLink.

Western, B. (2002). The impact of incarceration on wage mobility and inequality. *American Sociological Review, 67*(4), 526–546.

Western, B., Kling, J. R., & Weiman, D. F. (2001). The labor market consequences of incarceration. *Crime & Delinquency, 47*(3), 410–427.

White, M. D. (2002). Identifying situational predictors of police shootings using multivariate analysis. *Policing: An International journal of Police Strategies and Management, 25*(4), 726–751.

White, M. D., Fradella, H. F., & Coldren, J. R. (2015, August 11). Why police (and communities) need 'broken windows.' *The Crime Report*. Retrieved from http://www.thecrimereport.org/viewpoints/2015-08-why-police-and-communities-need-broken-windows

Wilkerson, I. (2013, September). No, you're not imagining it. *Essence, 44*, 132–137.

Williams, C. (2015, March 25). D.C. police chief Cathy L. Lanier urges empathy in policing. *The Washington Post*. Retrieved from https://www.washingtonpost.com/local/crime/dc-police-chief-cathy-l-lanier-urges-departments-to-incorporate-empathy/2015/03/25/78189830-d356-11e4-8fce-3941fc548f1c_story.html

Wilson, J. Q., & Kelling, G. (1982, March). Broken windows: The police and neighborhood safety. *The Atlantic*. Retrieved from http://www.theatlantic.com/magazine/archive/1982/03/broken-windows/304465/

Wood, M., Hales, J., Purdon, S., Sejersen, T., & Hayllar, O. (2009). *A test for racial discrimination in recruitment practice in British cities (Report No. 607)*. London, UK: National Centre for Social Research on behalf of the UK Department for Work and Pensions.

Woodcock, A., & Monteith, M. J. (2012). Forging links with the self to combat implicit bias. *Group Processes & Intergroup Relations, 16*(4), 445–461.

Index

© The Author(s) 2017   117
L.A. Fridell, *Producing Bias-Free Policing*,
SpringerBriefs in Translational Criminology, DOI 10.1007/978-3-319-33175-1

Printed by Printforce, the Netherlands